THE BRIDPORT

POETRY, SHORT STORIES A

CW00506015

JUDGES
Inua Ellams • Poetry
Tim Pears • Short Stories
Kathy Fish • Flash Fiction

First published in 2022 by Redcliffe Press Ltd
81g Pembroke Road, Bristol BS8 3EA
e: info@redcliffepress.co.uk
www.redcliffepress.co.uk

Follow us on Twitter @RedcliffePress
© the contributors

Follow The Bridport Prize:
Follow us on Twitter and Instagram @BridportPrize

www.bridportprize.org.uk
www.facebook.com/bridportprize

ISBN 978-1-915670-01-4

British Library Cataloguing-in-Publication Data
A catalogue record for this book is available from the British Library

Typeset in 10.5pt Times

Typeset by Addison Print Ltd, Northampton
Printed by Hobbs the Printers Ltd, Totton

Contents

Nothing short of brilliant

Which words make it onto a page is every writer's dilemma. When the form is short each word vies for attention like a line of siblings, hands raised, eyes bright, ever hopeful.

In these troubled times a short story, poem or work of flash fiction is a place of shelter from the world's unceasing noise. Characters, events and imagery move into our hearts, many never leave and their creative mark becomes a unique gift from writer to reader.

Thank you to all the writers featured here and to those who did not make it this time (please, don't give up). Writing is about sitting tight on the rollercoaster of rejection, laughing when the rain comes and pushing uphill against fear of failure.

It is also about taking a big leap to share your thoughts, hopes and dreams with others.

Reading the pieces entered into The Bridport Prize is a privilege. You trusted us with your words – that matters more than anything.

Buckle up and prepare to meet people, discover secrets and learn quiet truths from writers who had the kernel of an idea they would not, could not, let go.

Hold tight. It's sure to be a memorable ride.

The Bridport Prize Team

INUA ELLAMS

Poetry Report

Judging this year's Bridport Prize was a challenge. My other projects had overrun and spilled into the days I had reserved for the process, such that I struggled to find enough time to read and contemplate – at first. But as soon as I began, the importance of poetry – its particular offerings and the reasons for its hallowed place among the literary arts – recaptured my attention, grew within me, and out, to envelope the precious hours I spent among the verses of so many talented and passionate writers. Their voices would call to me as I slept, and I'd wake with their words in my ears.

There were poems about angels and champagne, prayers to the octopus, about care work, wind turbines and cameras, about field mice and domestic boredom, sonatas and blackbirds, about the many names for rain among many poems about grief and death. The wide range of topics covered, and the various forms, tonalities and textures demonstrated the growing democratisation of poetry, and the vibrant writing identities and communities creating important work.

I'd like to start my report by touching on the fantastic highly commended poems, beginning – in no particular order with:

'Working Debenhams' Late Shift', a gorgeous poem that begins as a critique of hyper–capitalist retail tradition, then grows to a tender portrait of a young woman's relationship with her father.

'Game', expertly and deftly recounts the grey areas of a relationship played out through social media, where in the final line, the writer asks us the readers our interpretation of the events "did he. did he use me."

In tightly written couplets, 'Townies' uses the group of city slickers visiting the countryside pop culture trope to comment on responsibility and power, on gods and mortality "But it's hard / for gods – they never get on".

'All My Bodies' which includes line "to bathe in oil and submit to massage without revulsion" is a powerful poem about self–reclamation, a woman coming to terms with, and owning the changes and transitions of her body throughout her life.

'New School' is a haunting, haunting, depth charge of a poem, a clever, subtle lamentation of a childhood death and the gaping whole left – a poem that grows with each reading.

'Telegraph Poles' reads like a nature poem, but it is a deep and curious, sonorous fragile capturing of telecommunications… "Tune in to electric blood that thrilled and sang / along the wire".

'David and Goliath' follows in the tradition of poems about sculptures. Picking out precise details of the marble Biblical hero, "if you could flatten the frown / and part the lips", it asks a simple question… what might David say about his current predicament?

As a fan of basketball, 'Watching the little sisters' leapt out to me for its precise commentary on the gender dynamics within the sport, but more importantly, for the watchful eye of its speaker as the young "practice defense, as women must".

'Remembrance' is a poem about a seemingly insignificant "shard" of a thing. By its use of repetition – though we never know what it is – the shard grows with importance and with language, much like how poetry works "Just a fragment… A tiny piece of plate or something".

And finally, 'Waiting Outside' another haunting poem that emotionally and powerfully conjures memories of the tireless work of medical professionals in its depiction of a lost surgical glove "a pale / hand scrabbling in the dust / for something lost".

In 3rd place, I chose – 'My Father's Fingernails'. Of the many emotive poems submitted about death, this poem uses what is often frowned at and discarded from the body as its starting point. The speaker finds "'a tiny / cache in his backyard on a stump under the pine" – foreshadowing the poem's ending, but along the journey, describing the father's habits. We learn he was a smoker, a private man, who kept his mysteries to himself, all of which explains the speaker's tender actions "I swept those trimmings / into my palm and brought my breath close, / as if blowing on embers". It is a tender work, that lifts in its closing line, pointing towards the circle of life.

'Scene in Media Res' took 2nd place. It is said, poetry and photography often serve the same function, and this poem serves that argument. The first lines declare its intention "The frozen present glitters like a frost / full of storefront manikins" and though it unfolds almost like a typical list poem, the writer's choices – what is drawn to our attention, and the formidable uses of line breaks, keeps us transfixed as we read of: spaghetti, birds, explosions, a couple, droplets of rain, all driving towards an unexpected, emotionally charged figure, alive and alone in the city.

Choosing an overall winner was exceptionally difficult. I was torn between two poems, 'My Father and I Drive to St. Louis for His Mother's Funeral, and I Can't Remember If We Brought Flowers' and 'After You Self-Medicate with Roethke's *The Waking* Read by Text–to–Speech App'.

The similarities are stark. Both poems have long titles, both deal with memory and cross–generational familial relationships, both use repetition as structural devices, both poems are prose poems, both require you to read by tumbling through and piecing together the narrative, and both poems being with a mother–figure.

'My Father and I...' comments on abuses of power by police officers, deftly conjuring the uncomfortable yet familiar scene with "I am asked to exit my vehicle / as if I had a choice / So there is a point in the journey when the frame holds".

'After You Self-Medicate...' comments on feminine interdependence and maternal love, with the line "you lift the baby who watches you with milk drunk eyes half closed and as you lay her in your daughter's arms".

Both poems have halting, startling imagery. In 'My Father and I...' "the hill stills / more or less / its green / & the dandelions become a haven / for the bees to stuff their pockets with gold" and in 'After You Self-Medicate...' "lullaby you once knew but now is a fragment of bees buzzing over the figs that have fallen as you lay in the shade". Both poems also reach suspenseful and emotionally charged cliff–hanger endings.

For these reasons, I could not choose one over the other, so chose both poems as joint winners of this year's Bridport Poetry prize. It is my belief they are in conversation with each other, and should be read together, that by their pairing, we glimpse the human spirit and expand our understandings of contemporary life.

TIM PEARS

Short Story Report

V. S. Pritchett, English master of the short story, wrote that a story "can be rather stark and bare unless you put in the right details. Details make stories human, and the more human a story can be, the better."

I was repeatedly reminded of Pritchett's dictum while reading the one hundred shortlisted entries for this year's Bridport Short Story Prize, which glittered with memorable detail.

The best art achieves two almost incompatible goals: an artist gives us their unique vision, yet in doing so enlarges and illuminates the wider world we all share. Such is the case with the following ten *Highly Commended* stories.

Caravan
Five men drive their camels across featureless, harsh steppe. Camels loaded with opium. Hard, desperate, determined men, each one etched in words as if in stone. On they drive, through the sand and wind, towards their misbegotten destinies. What a story.

Focaccia
Subtitled *A brief tale of infatuation in the modern age*, to which there's little to add except to say that the tale hopscotches from paragraph to paragraph with tremendous wit and elan.

Hatches Before They Chicken
Lena demands her daughter Katy and boyfriend Harry's compulsory attendance at her seventy-eighth birthday party, in the Polish Community Centre. The party is an opportunity for Lena to ridicule and castigate her guests. This eccentric immigrant is at the centre of rich comedy that surely extends outside the story.

Seventeen Weeks
Bianca is pregnant, but is there something wrong with the baby? The author takes us into her mind, digressing, obsessing, threatening to unravel yet fiercely intelligent, and fascinating to travel with into a medical, emotional circle of hell.

Pollinate
Amber and her young colleagues work in a vast orchard. What are they doing, as they move around? Are they dancing? Gradually we understand that they are pollinating the fruit trees, humans mimicking the actions of the bees that have gone. An outlandish scenario the author renders entirely credible.

I need you to be Harold
A classical short story. The fey narrator, a modern day superfluous man, goes out of town for a weekend away and is drawn into a hare-brained, identity-swapping drama, which is also a lovely consideration of our sense of ourselves as substantial beings.

Alice
Ian, the narrator, gets a call at two in the morning from his volatile ex-girlfriend. She needs rescuing. He responds. Does she really need rescuing? Does he really need to respond? The author takes us on their subsequent journey through the night with verve and brio.

1967
New York. A man meets a woman in Grand Central Station. The identities of these people, where they're from, what they're doing, and the wider relationships in their lives, is fed to us so subtly, line by line. This writer is an angler, drawing us in.

Monumenta
A female chief executive of a construction company flees Germany for her mother and brother at home in Belgrade, after a terrible accident for which she might be responsible, or at least blamed. Is she in flight from disaster, from the future, from success, from modern Europe? In flight to refuge, the past, the primitive? Real, earthy characters yet political-cultural resonance, what more can one ask for?

The Last Year the Ice Lake Sang
A man lies in a hospital bed, in a strange clinic somewhere in Germany. His night-shift nurse, Heike, tells him about the ice lake, and conceives a plan to take him there. Gradually it dawns on the reader who this man is. A magical story.

Any of these *Highly Commended* stories could have made the top three. Judgement of work of such quality is not merely subjective but almost random. Still, the choice had to be made.

In third place is *The Truth About The Lies People Told About Cattle*, an audacious, innovatively structured yet highly readable, worldly story about geopolitics, international trade and cultural difference, featuring a cow falling from the sky and sinking a boat. Quite brilliant.

In second place, *46A to Dun Laoghaire* follows Annie through a manic evening with her troubled, unstable, intoxicating girlfriend Lorna who, from one moment to another, gets Annie in trouble while simultaneously liberating her. An exhilarating ride for both Annie and the reader, the theme is thrillingly embodied on every page.

In first place is *This is Going to be Huge*. Sasha's best friend in childhood, Blair, inexplicably betrays her. In time Sasha gets over it. She builds a life, a career, a family. Blair is long gone, yet remains, a faint unresolved ghost in Sasha's mind. Then they meet again... A beautifully modulated story about character, with clues to the personality of those drawn towards cultish insanity, and a most moving exploration of the needs friendship can probably never fulfil.

KATHY FISH

Flash Fiction Report

Quietly or not-so-quietly incendiary. Expansive. Evocative. Containing more story, more complexity than seems possible in the limited space it inhabits, flash fiction demands us to sit up and take notice. By its sheer brevity, it announces its urgency on the page, demands that we pay close attention to every single word.

And we do. The best flash fiction works this kind of magic. It may take as little as two minutes to read, but we come away feeling as though we've read a novel. The best examples of the form are immersive and precise and deeply compelling. Much more than simply a shorter short story, often employing the tools of poetry, flash fiction is its own distinct literary form.

The late U.S. politician Ann Richards famously said Ginger Rogers had to do everything her dance partner Fred Astaire did, only backwards and wearing high heels. That is the challenge of the flash writer, to accomplish what short story writers and novelists do, but with a fraction of words at their disposal.

For the Bridport Flash Fiction Prize, writers were limited to a mere two hundred and fifty words, at the lower end of the flash fiction range. These writers were not only dancing backwards in high heels, they were teetering on a tight rope. Flash this short requires precision and daring and if needs be, a willingness to work outside traditional structures and rules.

My thanks to the team of initial readers who made the tough decisions necessary to winnow down the submissions to the ninety-three I was honored to read and judge. Any judge of art is of course, subjective. Ultimately what made the stories you're about to read stand out for me was mastery of craft and originality. This is what guided me as I made what turned out to be quite daunting decisions from a high standard of submissions.

All of the Highly Commended stories moved or delighted me in some way. "Falling Woman" tells a universal story in a fresh and layered, poetic manner. "Valentine's Day" is told via a series of images that build to create a powerful overall picture. "That Time You Went to Space" is a voice-driven piece that captures a devastating moment around a dinner table in a single sentence. "Autopsy of a Mother" is surprising and original, both tender and sad. And "The Life of Fibonacci, Shaped to Resemble a Galaxy or Pine Cone" is a dazzling display of form.

I found the three prize winning stories simply brilliant, captivating, haunting. Even after multiple readings, these stories stayed with me. Indeed they will always stay with me.

Third Prize winner "In the Museums of Heaven and Hell," is an aimed and powerful piece, unique and incisive, with a final sentence that lands hard.

"Yesterday, They Crossed the Elbe" won Second Prize and is a striking, cinematically told story that will forever haunt me. The point of view alone is one of the most original I have ever read.

The flash I chose for First Prize, "Some creatures trapped in ice" clobbered me on first reading and every read thereafter. The very best flash fiction has an epic feel to it. Something urgent and compelling and utterly new. This flash was all that and more. All three of the top prize winners are stories that will stay with me a very long time, but especially this one.

Warmest congratulations to the winners. I am in awe of the skill and daring and passion you brought to your work. And to the readers, I am confident you will enjoy these tiny masterpieces as much as I did.

ROBERTA BEARY

After You Self-Medicate with Roethke's *The Waking* Read by Text-to-Speech App

You're in one of your weepy moods and your mother turns her sea green eyes and lifts your baby from your arms and says did you ever notice her little heart shaped face so like yours and you say no but now that you mention it and you smile as your mother hands you back your baby who opens to your breast and afterwards watches you with milk drunk eyes half closed as you unlatch and when you turn your mother is gone and the baby is sleeping so you lay her on the lighthouse quilt while you answer the doorbell and sign for yet another package and your mother is somewhere you can't see no matter how many corners you scan as you lift the lighthouse quilt and *what falls away is always and is near* and the baby you hold looks nothing like your baby well maybe a little in the curve of her mouth or the way one eye is slightly higher than the other or perhaps it is the heart shape of the tiny face that is somewhat familiar in her dress of yellow polka dots and just then your daughter asks you for her baby and *what falls away is always and is near* and you lift the baby who watches you with milk drunk eyes half closed and as you lay her in your daughter's arms the lighthouse quilt slips to the floor and the doorbell rings you sign for yet another package you tell yourself the ache is for that long ago stray your mother brought home how he followed your every forbidden step and you feel yourself get weepy in a way your daughter never does not even when your mother died but she did a lovely job with the memorial photos that one of the three of you in matching yellow polka dots and *what falls away is always and is near* and you do your timed breathing standing at the window where the magnolia petals brush the rain or is it the other way around which is something your mother would know and you tell yourself that when people say weave the unspoken words into a letter to read at the graveside they don't know what the hell they're talking about and the magnolia unfurls its petals as the rain sings a lullaby you once knew but now is a fragment of bees buzzing over the figs that have fallen as you lay in the shade of your mother's yellow polka dots while you wait for her to say something momentous but she only asks for her reading glasses and the two nurses erase her name from the whiteboard and you go back to your timed breathing until your daughter says would you mind holding the baby and her sea green eyes look weepy like a memory tucked inside your pocket and you lift the baby from your daughter's arms and as the lighthouse quilt slips the baby unfurls her fists and smiles a crescent moon and you say did you ever notice the baby's little heart shaped face so like yours and your daughter says no but now that you mention it and you hear your mother calling from inside your other pocket and *what falls away is always and is near.*

CHAUN BALLARD

My Father and I Drive to St. Louis for His Mother's Funeral, and I Can't Remember If We Brought Flowers

There is a story in a journey / a son takes / with his father / that circles back to a field of flowers / that stays a field of flowers / only in name / & because our eyes pass them along a road / there is a point in a journey when all the years blur the same / Meaning / the details it took to get there / & the details it takes to get back— / & there is a point in a journey when a volta pivots inside a narrative / when a father turns the wheel over to his son / & this is the moment when a father releases his child / to the wind / & the boy learns to fail / or the boy learns to fly / & we desire shade from our oak trees / where the robins watch their nests / & sure / this could be a story about how a parent never rests / once his hands relinquish control / & my father never slept along the journey / (though I'd seen him doze) / & we mostly ate fast food / & paused for gas / So there is a point in the journey when the journey becomes a hill / a literal slope / somewhere between a field / & Texas / where our bodies enter a highpoint / & there is a tension / & / peripheral to a son / & / peripheral to a father / are likely flowers blowing in a wind / that could be from anywhere / we could be anyone / & I could ask for anything / So there is a point in a journey where I become a magic lamp / & my father becomes a field of wildflowers / & the thing about a magic lamp is / how gently the hands tremble / once the wheels turn slowly onto the shoulder / So there is a point in the journey / where I pull off the road / & I am asked to exit my vehicle / as if I had a choice / So there is a point in the journey when the frame holds / & the hill stills / more or less its green / & the dandelions become a haven / for the bees to stuff their pockets with gold / & / by this standard / my father can no longer be likened to a field / of wildflowers / & / the thing about a magic lamp / is / I only get three wishes / & my father is being cross-examined / as I make use of them all / So there is a point in a journey when / *who lives to tell the tale* / & / *from what point of view* / become central to the climax / & if the man toting the gun has a third-person limited / & if the plane in the sky has a god's point of view / I am all out of wishes / & the thing about a journey is / at some point it becomes a prayer / & what I mean is / *from this point on* / & the man with the gun is all about the math / & see / what should be viewed as routine / does not start out that way / & what is likely to be believed / requires / neither of us / So there is a point in a journey when it ends the way it begins / with that which appears different / on the surface / & the man holding the gun wants to know / if our stories corroborate / & to think / all of this came from my being / too relaxed / from allowing my foot to coast down a hill / while I mistook a field of dandelions to be a field of wildflowers / & that was my mistake / & the plane that was said to have calculated my duration / to distance (before the age of drones) / is not put to a vote / So there is a point in a journey when I return to the math / & I have never been one for arithmetic / so forgive me if my story does not add up / I leave this problem for you to resolve / since I know you will work through my miscalculation / & the thing about a miscalculation / is how a journey could end / & the thing about a journey ending is / how easy it is to misfire / & what I mean is / how easy it is to begin with a field of flowers / & end / with no flowers at all

DAMEN O'BRIEN

Scene in Media Res

The frozen present glitters like a frost
full of storefront manikins, poised
between steps, absurd in their candid
frieze, full of fallen things: wine glasses
nudged into suspension, their red tongues
licking air; plates mooned to fracture
and spillage, stiff in their starburst of
spaghetti; a startle of pigeons, lurching
or rising, caught in hard air. I've
wandered these empty full streets, seen
the hot bullets hover, the ball seek its
catcher, the birds in their amber, the
imminent accident, fire flaring and ghastly,
the explosion's penumbra, in one passed
street, the crumple wave of pressure as two
cars collided, but nothing would answer,
obdurate and fatal, nothing would turn,
adamant as steel, everything was falling
though nothing had fallen: the couple,
sprawling onto their bed in one hushed
apartment; the standing curtain of droplets
in another room's shower. Things want
the conclusions they are given: waiters
shouldering the double kitchen doors,
or that man I was, frozen, half standing,
the wine glass, the pasta, in endless poured
portraits, everything on pause but that one
woman leaving, the only movement, always
and pitiless, her dress, her back, walking away.

LANCE LARSEN

My Father's Fingernails

He left them around the house in slivered piles:
on his nightstand, beside the tub, at the battered
desk where he tied midges and hoppers and sinking
nymphs, marinating himself in melancholy
jazz. Weeks after we buried him, I found a tiny
cache in his backyard on a stump under the pine,
an accumulation of calcium and trimmed
cuticles, a tiny cairn placed just so for the next ant
or beetle on trek. Some fingernails ridged
and stained as if with nicotine. There were other
offerings as well, whorled and split, yellowed
like rinds. And I realized he had slipped off
his shoes in that shaded corner to work
on his twisted toes. What a fastidious oh so private
pile of keratin. I swept those trimmings
into my palm and brought my breath close,
as if blowing on embers, to clear away dust
and pollen. Now it was just him in my hand.
What allegories in aging, travails in frailty
I held I'll never know. How the body fails
but continues to drag us gingerly along? I never
told my mom. I knelt. With my free hand,
I cleared away strewn pine needles, then scratched
back the earth. Into that furrow I sifted what
was left of my father, as if planting something
stolen, as if keeping secrets from the prying sky.

NICOLE ADABUNU

game

you got published by The New Yorker & i thought that was hot. blah blah. when i'm easy i'm easy.
tonight i let an anyone goosebump me. tonight i pick you.

you come as the sun begins to down. iowa bothers me. i tell you that at night i pretend
the lights outside are new york city. i think therefore it is. perfect. i am perfect
at pretending things don't bother me. watch this.

we drink & drink & drink. i should have stopped me. starlight dances through the window dances
through your skin. how could i not reach. you made it too easy. you say *can i ask*
a stupid question. can i kiss you. can i kiss you. i give a stupid answer.

what i want i get. 3 hours later. there's no part of you i didn't twitch. you. skyscraped over me. staring.
i've never seen a grown man so hungry. *you're trouble*, you say. *addicting. perfect.* you say i'm all that
& this & these. you nod into the heat of me. god. under you i feel so new york lights.

do i still look pretty from this angle

finally finished. you tell me your age. something in the night shifts. desire walks back home.
but the hunger hasn't left your eyes. there's so much of you on my floor. so much ~~healing~~
cleaning to do. so so much cleaning.

your facebook status says you're engaged. out of courtesy for your partner i lick me
off your lips.

you sit next to me on the bed & i feel the years between us. i want to hide. you say you don't care
about age. you hold my hand. you call me pretty.

next to you i feel more prey than pretty. there is so little distance between the two. two letters
holding hands. take away the hands. take away the holding. pretty prey pretty prey pretty prey
pretty prey prey prey

alcohol blurs the distance between two bodies.

reader. can i ask a stupid question. did he. did he use me.

20

FREYA BANTIFF

Working Debenhams' Late Shift

Sheffield floods, November 7th 2019

If this is a preview of the end of the world,
my phone is a reel of red alerts and head office
still don't want us to go home. They say things like,
we can't tell until it happens and then all the buses
are cancelled. I count eight raindrops per second
from the single stamp window in the stockroom
by the clicked parcels that won't be collected.
An umbrella shouts up, *it's a hell of a night*
and I believe it, walking faster as I set off under
what once were streetlamps – now unidentified
flickering objects. Dad texts, *I'm coming through town,*
where are you. I say, *I've passed the pyjama-striped*
cinema, am stood by the undressed trees and manikins,
it's cold and then I spot his bald head like the dome
of a temple. Like the splashed shine of a boar snout
polished bronze in Florence. If you rubbed it,
it promised your return. *We'll have toast*
when we get home, he says as we slip into step
and a silence thick and buttery. A student takes
her bicycle for a walk, then a swim. A wrung dishcloth
of a spaniel is carried. A tent floats upside-down.
Nice weather for ducks, a man calls and laughs
like a thunderclap. All I know is my dad rolls up
his trouser legs, wades knee-high into the underpass
which thrums like the dark centre of my gran's
macular degeneration where straight lines run crooked
and there are only eddies of the peripheral.
And I worry I am missing what's important.
Yet he hums, *can't go over it, can't go under it…*
and when the asteroid strikes, when the locusts plague,

when the angels come down with minted rage
and inexorable glory I know they'll have to stay
their blazing hands for the father who waits
for his daughter while she empties out her boots.

JANET DEAN

All My Bodies

Inside my hated body my loathed body the body of bags of sugar stuck
to my belly of orange peel drying on my face of knees clicking of eyes
seeping   the woman whose jeans feel loose whose dress discovers
how to drape who can cross her legs   whose arms sit tight on an open
car window whose hair is melting   a woman able to bear contractions
or not to bear   but to survive   to use her breasts to feed   her hands to
nurture   a woman still brave enough to let a man see her body in over
head light   to delight in her own agility   to bathe in oil and submit to
massage without revulsion   a girl in hot pants bikini   knee length
boots   with teeth whose only gap is in the middle   a girl who starts
with 32A   who retains the idea of her chubby childhood   the
freckly speckly girl who reddens easily   a girl who wishes she looked
like any other   a girl with a fringe her dad cut badly   a child with
bleeding eczema in the crooks of her knees   who sneezes all summer
    a child well-loved and cuddled but still unsure   a 10lb baby who
        pinned her struggling mother to the floor.

JENNY DOUGHTY

Watching the little sisters

The teenage boys have gone to a back yard
somewhere in the neighborhood to hang out
behind a garage, pass around a joint,
and now I see their little sisters
take a turn at the basketball hoop
on the sidewalk: fifth graders in shorts
or old leggings starting to climb above
their slim ankles, T shirts still printed
with unicorns, still flat across their chests.

To watch them is to travel back in time
before the uniform of gender
fell across my shoulders, before the weight
of breasts and male gaze boxed out freedom
even more than the shot clock of childhood,
before bleeding and the inescapable
decades to come of decisions wrapped up
in owning a grown woman's body.
There are so many ways of being fouled.

I never see them alone; they huddle
in pairs or groups of three or four. I hear
their high voices chattering, their laughter,
before the basketball bops on asphalt.
They practice defense, as women must,
dodging side to side to block a shot.
They jump high in front of the girl with the ball,
flinging their arms into the air, T-shirts
riding up over their bare bellies.

24

BEATRICE GARLAND

Telegraph Poles

Sometimes on a walk with the grownups
I'd trail behind to lean my face against
a warm brown splintery trunk; sniff at
the creosote, gaze at the arteries that dipped
and soared in swags between each pole;
tune in to electric blood that thrilled and sang
along the wire; the endless adult discourse,
their indecipherable accounts of
triumph and disaster, love and death.

NAIRN KENNEDY

New School

Time, like the Mafia, leaves few witnesses;
maybe the fire hydrant with the missing plate
or the silent row of bollards watched it happen,
while the bungalow winced and covered
the wideness of its eyes.

We met on the Town Hall stage, gladiators
of opposing teams in the Road Safety Quiz;
your mother sat side by side with mine,
brimming that we'd be pupils in the next school,
that we might be friends.

When I rolled up in August, checked the lists,
there you were in print in class 1A, neatly typed
by a school which didn't know
about the cul-de-sac, reversing bus, the lack
of vision at the back.

PAUL MATTHEWS

Waiting Outside

It was not only dry leaves
swirling across the car park.

The November wind kept
tossing a surgical glove

over and over. It was a pale
hand scrabbling in the dust

for something lost, a body
to belong to.

One moment it flipped
sinister as if seeding some

further pestilence;
then, as the wind paused,

I saw how disconsolate
the thing was and wanted

those dark leaves to cradle
that stillborn emptiness.

KATE RUTTER

David and Goliath

If you could cool your palm on the marble
of his lower back, slip your fingers into his
slingshot hand and pry it open, if you could push
a knuckle into the nest between his collar bones,

if you could flatten the frown
and part the lips, flat-hand the belly's hill,
the hooded navel, the cock, if you could lift

his front foot to trace the river of a vein,
the rutted edge of a toe-nail, he would smile,
relax onto a solid back foot and speak of the odds,
of courage, of the smallness of a pebble.

DAVID SWANN

Townies

When the bullocks chased us, we sprinted
hell for leather over the fell, our teenage-cool

in pieces as we climbed a farmer's fence,
the throne that restored our divinity.

How thick those lumbering beasts looked
with their ear-tags and mud-caked hinds!

We cobbed rocks at their shit, awarding points
for direct hits, then struggled to agree scores

so threatened to brain each other with stones
before brooding in a fold by the beck,

where driftwood had piled in a ditch,
rotted and black, as out of place as we felt,

out there in the wilds with our townie hungers.
The fish saved us. Sticklebacks, fierce as coins

in the peaty water. We cupped our hands
carefully and put them in cow-troughs

before returning to rip weeds from the beck,
in a rare fit of care. But when, hours later,

we came back, squabbling, hands green
and dripping, we found a dull brown flotilla,

belly-up in the troughs. Not fish now. Twigs.
We trudged home, watched by the bullocks,

David Swann

now sullen and motionless in their pasture,
as if news had spread of the reckless powers

we'd brought up from town. But it's hard
for gods – they never get on. Wearied by trials,

and glad to see the back of each other,
we shut our front doors and climbed the stairs

to enter that field between two states,
where dreams moved like beasts to the fence.

CATH WILLS

Remembrance

Just a shard
Came upon a shard
Stumbled on a small shard
Dug it up while weeding
A square shard of crockery
Almost a square

Just a fragment
Unearthed the pattern
A fragment of a pattern
A tiny piece of plate or something
Coughed up in the mud
A fragment of a bigger something

TRENT ENGLAND

This is Going to be Huge

It was a small thing, but it mattered. On the night that Blair was supposed to go to Sasha's house for a sleepover, she called to cancel. Blair coughed into the line, and when she spoke, her voice sounded like tape stretching off its spool. She said it felt like strep, and that her mom was going to try to get her into an urgent care clinic first thing in the morning. After the call, Sasha went downstairs, feeling a little glum, a little put out. Her parents were watching something they'd rented, one of the *Lethal Weapon* sequels, and they paused the tape. Sasha told them what had happened, and her dad reached for his wallet and gave her cash so she could go to the mall and have dinner in the food court.

She wandered from store to store at a quick pace, as though she were rushing through a to-do list, ticking off each store after briefly looking around. With the cash from her father, she bought the newest Smashing Pumpkins CD as well as a Free Tibet bumper sticker that she planned to pin to the cork board on her bedroom wall even though she didn't know exactly where Tibet was and why it should be freed. There was enough money left over for a chocolate caramel shake and she sipped it slowly while she sat in a massage chair at Brookstone. An employee asked if she had any questions about the chair, but Sasha didn't answer him because, at that moment, she saw Blair. She was walking out of an Abercrombie across from the Brookstone, flanked by two tall juniors named Becks and Krista. Sasha ran across the way and called out to her friend. Blair turned around, red-faced, and coughed, a little less convincingly than she had over the phone. She told Sasha that she was still sick but that coming to the mall had been a last-minute thing — specifically to get a fruit smoothie, and she'd happened to run into her friends when she was there.

Sasha didn't believe this story, but pretended to because she didn't want to make a scene and there was still the possibility that Blair was telling the truth. For the second time that night she told Blair that she hoped she felt better soon, and when they said goodbye it was tense and awkward and Sasha wanted to die. Walking out of the mall, she felt angrier with each step, and she drove home whispering her side of an imaginary conversation. She went straight to her room and lay in bed and listened to her new CD and every once in a while she looked over at the phone that never rang with an apology from Blair, and it was the first weekend since she and Sasha were eleven that they did not talk on the phone.

* * *

A lifetime passed, and then it was Monday morning. Blair, between classes, ducked into a nearby bathroom when she saw Sasha walking toward her down the hall. At lunch, Sasha decided to eat in the newspaper office instead of the cafeteria, and get a head start on the layout for next week's issue. An annoying girl named Casey, who somehow found the time to be a part of every club and was also the editor of the school newspaper, walked in and sat at a computer next to Sasha. After a while, Casey looked over and said that she was sorry.

'Sorry for what?'

'I'm sorry about what happened between you and Blair. I heard she changed lockers.' Casey opened a can of grape soda. 'I had a big fight with my best friend in middle school, and it really sucked.'

Sasha was surprised to hear this about the lockers, and had a hard time finding something to say back. Soon, though, she asked Casey where she'd heard this — about Blair moving lockers. Casey shrugged and returned to looking at her computer monitor.

'Everywhere, I guess.'

Later that day, when Sasha walked into Algebra II and saw that all the seats around Blair were taken, she sat in the only empty desk, which was in the back of the classroom, by one of the broad windows, where sunlight bathed the left side of her face. Miss Ledbetter chalked up the board with equations, and then she guided everyone through a lesson on page 199 in their textbooks. She lectured while she worked. Algebra, she said, is about the reunion of broken parts. She was known around the school to be a spiritual person, and in class she made numbers sound like mystical agents in a game designed by God. Algebra is about making things whole again. We are performing grace with variables and functions. Sasha's mind was elsewhere, though. She couldn't get over the fact that her best friend had lied to her, but she felt powerless to do anything about it. She was forced to either accept Blair's version of how she came to be at the mall with Becks and Krista, or become the villain by taking issue with it.

By the end of the school year, they were no longer speaking to one another. And while Sasha wasn't surprised to hear, after the fact, that Blair had thrown an end-of-year pool party at her house, it still hurt. There was an air of finality to the lack of an invitation. Sasha thought about the things at Blair's house that belonged to her — a pair of old eyeglasses that she kept around in case she lost a contact, her Adidas sliders, half a bottle of concealer cream, and her Guess beach towel. She wondered if Blair had played Sasha's Fugees CD at the party, or if they were all drinking some of the orange Gatorades that Blair's mom Julia kept in the fridge just for her. Were people talking openly about the fact that Sasha wasn't at the party? That Sasha and Blair weren't as good of friends as they used to be, or if they were still friends at all?

Over the summer, she got a job as a hostess at a Mexican restaurant called El Potro, and after a couple of weeks was promoted to waitress; the employees were always quitting or they were being fired for too many no-shows. One Friday during lunch, Blair walked into the restaurant accompanied by a group of girls Sasha hadn't seen before, and the hostess, by sheer luck, sat them in a different section. Sasha took her break and hid in the kitchen, where she could watch Blair. Sasha had heard that Blair's parents were sending her to a new school in the fall, and that she would no longer be a Tiger. She already looked like a different person; she had bleached her hair and she was wearing clothes Sasha had never seen. She carried herself like someone else; her body language and even her laugh were unrecognizable. She seemed to have a new level of cool and confidence, and commanded the attention of the others at the table in a way that seemed foreign to Sasha. Sasha was paralyzed. What had become of her old friend. She couldn't leave her post in the kitchen, couldn't stop watching Blair — until Blair slowly turned around and looked in Sasha's direction. They made eye contact for a brief moment, a second of a second, and then Sasha panicked, backed out of the kitchen and hid in the manager's office until she was certain that Blair was gone.

* * *

After high school, Sasha attended college in Western Pennsylvania, and she heard that Blair had stayed in Boston for college, though no one could say for certain which school. Sasha joined Facebook when membership expanded from Ivy League-only schools to anyone with a .edu email address, and the first person she searched for was Blair. But there was no Blair Lanham on Facebook, not even an Alexandra Blair Lanham, her full name, or Alexandra Lanham or even Alex Lanham. Sasha was hungry for information. She logged in to Yahoo Messenger, but Blair's old screen name was inactive. She trawled MySpace, Xanga, and then LiveJournal, but Blair didn't have accounts with any of these social networks. Then she tried looking Blair up by using Yahoo and Google, but both search engines only led to a web page for the school where Blair had attended her last two years of high school, specifically an index of the track and field athletes and their meet times, the names accompanied by blank squares with red Xs where there had once been photographs.

Finally, Sasha decided to send her an email, to the only email address that she'd known Blair to ever have. The message was short, cordial and curious. She wrote that she'd been wondering how her old friend was doing, and, if she had the time, to write back and tell her how life had been treating her. She hit send, and – seconds later – it pinged back. Blair's email address no longer existed. And for a long time, that was the end of that.

After college, Sasha moved back to Massachusetts and got a job working for a personnel firm. She shared an apartment in Brookline with a girl named Adina and a lot of IKEA furniture, and she felt like she was back at college, with the division of chores and Adina's orderly labeling of all the food, laundry soap and toiletries. At night, when it was quiet, and when the windows were raised, she could hear the green line trolley from a couple streets away, and it comforted her. She didn't particularly care for living in Boston, but she wanted the city close by, just in case. This dictated where she would live for the rest of her adult life, and every apartment and house after the one on Garrison Road were always city-adjacent, even after she was married and had two children and at thirty-six had witnessed all of her old friends move an hour or more away from the city, decamping to bigger houses and lots of land on the south shore or the Cape. She wanted to remain close to Boston, but could never say why.

* * *

And then Sasha heard something about Blair that was impossible to believe.

One night, she was having after-work drinks with people in her office — a social event that she usually turned down. But that night, her daughters happened to be staying over at friends' houses and Grant was in the basement working on his newest batch of home-brewed beer. Sasha hadn't wanted to spend the evening eating dinner by herself on the couch, so she said yes to work drinks, which she now regretted as she stood shoulder-to-shoulder in a trendy bar downtown barely able to hear her colleagues. She leaned in closer. Daughter-in-private-school Jamie was talking to marathon-runner Jamie about a compositing initiative she wanted to implement at the office. And then marathon-runner Jamie began to compare the cost of composting companies in Boston, because, she said, she and her husband had recently looked into this themselves. How was it possible, Sasha thought, that the people she worked with were even more boring after having alcohol? Her mind wandered, and she fantasized about walking out of the bar without explanation. What would her colleagues say. And what would happen if she turned her phone off and walked around the city, aimless, for hours. What kind of people would she meet. What if she went home to a different house, and a different life.

There was a lull in the conversation, and Sasha excused herself to the bar to get another glass of wine. While she waited to get the bartender's attention, she heard someone say her name. She looked in the direction of her colleagues, but heard a voice to her right. Sasha turned, but didn't recognize the woman talking to her.

'Hey! It's Gabby. Gabby Frye?'

The double-barred doors of memory opened, and there she was: Gabby, driving her white Mustang with the top down; Gabby, arguing in the hallway with Aaron, her longtime off-and-on-again boyfriend; Gabby on stage at graduation sticking out her tongue between her fingers. The two women embraced, and Sasha apologized for not recognizing her right away.

Gabby tugged at her own hair.

'Well, it's fair. I wasn't this blonde back in the day.'

They caught each other up on their lives. Gabby was also here with friends from work, and she lived close by, in a high-rise in the West End. She was divorced and childless, and she didn't ask if Sasha was married or had kids. They took turns listing off the people they still talked to from the old days, but it was an uneventful swap of information; both women revealed themselves to be bad about staying in touch with friends from high school and ambivalent about social media. Finally, Sasha asked the question that had been nagging her.

'Do you ever hear from Blair Lanham?'

'No, but I did hear something interesting recently.' Gabby took a sip from her cocktail. 'I heard she'd joined a cult.'

Sasha laughed politely and Gabby insisted she was serious.

'I recently ran into – do you remember Sarah Moore? – anyway, she told me that, apparently, Blair had been living with some weird group in Vermont for a while that had, like, taken over her life or something. Anyway, she said that there had been an intervention and lawyers and everything, and now Blair's living back at home with her parents, who have, like, a conservatorship over her. It's all really sad.'

Someone from Gabby's group was calling to her, and she told Sasha that she should get back to her friends. They made tentative plans to get coffee one of these days and said they'd find each other on Facebook. But Sasha knew that they would not get coffee and they would never see each other again, unless it was by accident. Sasha and Gabby had never been friends in the first place, and owed each other nothing. They had only known one another because they had been thrown together at the same place and time, and saying hello tonight at a downtown bar was an obligation to the past. It was as if they'd been veterans of the same war, and were compelled by an old code to pause and say hello.

After they parted ways, Sasha couldn't stop thinking about what Gabby had told her. It was like hearing that Blair had joined the military and was now a high-ranking officer. Or that Blair had robbed a bank and was now in federal prison. It lingered in her mind after she had gotten home and changed into a t-shirt and sleep pants and drank half a bottle of Grant's newest pilsner. She pretended to show interest in the various label designs he was working on, but what she was thinking about was what Gabby had told her, and how it made her feel. She was surprised by her reaction, because it wasn't her business what Blair was doing with her life, and she wished that it could remain that way. After all, she thought, it was *Blair* who had transferred schools and disappeared off the face of the earth, and it was *Blair* who had been a bad friend. But this feeling of unease continued into the weekend and the weeks that followed. At work, at the grocery store, at one of her daughters' soccer games, she couldn't help but dwell on what Gabby had told her, despite the fact that she shouldn't have cared. It should have been one of those things that someone tells you that you shrug off. But it was about Blair, so it mattered.

* * *

For Halloween, Sasha and Grant dressed up as Frankenstein's monster and Bride of Frankenstein, and sat on the front porch with an ice bucket full of Grant's beers. Children walked up and helped themselves to candy from a bowl that sat on a bale of hay, leaving Sasha and Grant to drink and talk uninterrupted. And they talked about how nice it was to talk. Even though Josie and Quinn were older now, there was still little time for Sasha and Grant to have a real conversation. He opened up about a problem he was having at school with one of his students, a boy named Jacob who was disruptive, and who picked on other kids, but apparently had responded to Grant's sternness by telling his mother that Grant was singling him out in class, humiliating him. Now the mother was angry, she was what Grant called capital-I Involved. The administration's response had put him in a double bind, he told her, and it was the reason he'd not been sleeping well. Sasha saw in his green-painted face how difficult it had been to share this. It wasn't often that Grant talked about work, and she was moved by this revelation. When there was a break between trick-or-treaters, she decided to open up, too. She told him about a childhood friend of hers who, if you can believe it, had been part of a cult. Grant was astonished, and it distracted him from the blues of his own story. He said he'd never heard this happening to anyone he knew. He asked the basic questions. Sasha said that she'd fallen out of touch with Blair the summer before junior year, and that they never heard from each other again. She didn't tell him about the lie that Blair had told, and the days of avoidance that followed. Decades later, bringing it up would have seemed as if she were holding a grudge. It had taken her some time – and having girls of her own – but she now understood that what had happened between her and Blair wasn't uncommon. And she also understood that the end of their friendship hadn't entirely been Blair's fault.

Grant asked why she'd never mentioned this friend before. She said that Blair had been one of those people you forget about, until someone brings them to mind, and then you can't stop thinking about them. He said that he had a few friends like that. College friends, an old boss, the brother of an ex-girlfriend. After a while, he and Sasha were both quiet.

And then she said, 'I think I'm gonna go see her.'

* * *

She still remembered the number to the landline at the Lanhams' house. It was lodged deep in her memory like old commercial jingles and the feeling of her first kiss. Blair's mother answered the phone almost immediately. Sasha reintroduced herself, and Julia responded by laughing, as though it had been only yesterday that she was there, and told her that she remembered her.

Sasha asked to speak with Blair, and Julia said without hesitation that Blair couldn't talk on the phone, but that Sasha was welcome to come over to the house anytime. She said that Blair could use the company, and that she herself and Mike would love to see her. Sasha asked if the next day was okay, maybe after work. Julia said she would make chicken parmesan, that she remembered how much Sasha used to love it.

The driveway had been repaved and the house was painted a different shade of blue, but pulling up to the Lanhams' house still felt like coming home. Inside, she was embraced by Blair's parents. She looked around and took a deep breath, inhaling the scent of a previous life. The house still smelled like oatmeal; it was permanently a part of the fabric of the house, caked into the curtains and carpeting. Sasha removed her shoes, a force of habit, and placed them next to a pair of faded red Converse low tops — Blair's, she guessed. Sasha marveled at being back in their house, a place she never thought she'd see again, and her obvious delight seemed to please Mike and Julia. They asked about her life now, and Sasha told them about the company she worked for, and she told them about her daughters and about her husband. Julia lowered her voice and whispered that she was proud of her.

Down the hall, in the direction of Blair's room, a door opened and then closed. Sasha heard soft footsteps approaching, and then Blair walked out. She was thin, her hair was short and she wore a loose-fitting gray sweatshirt that said Williams College in purple letters.

The two women held each other's gaze for a moment.

'Sosh?'

After dinner, Sasha and Blair excused themselves to Blair's bedroom. Not much about the room had changed in the past two decades; there were still ticket stubs and photographs and award ribbons in the vanity mirror. A poster for the movie *Romeo + Juliet* still hung on the wall, its little tears exactly where Sasha had remembered.

They sat on the floor, backs against the bed.

'I can't believe twenty years ago was twenty years ago,' Blair said.

'It's surreal to be back here.'

'When my parents told me I had a surprise visitor, I wouldn't have ever guessed it was you. But I'm glad it was you.'

Sasha ran her palms over the familiar piling of the carpet.

'I feel like we should be watching Ethan Hawke movies and eating Taquitos.'

'I think my parents still have all my old tapes somewhere.'

'So are they in charge of everything about your life?'

'Some things are my own. Like, I choose what I wear, and I read whatever I want, even though I don't always feel like reading. But that's about it. And group therapy is about the only place I go without one of my parents there with me. So, I never miss a session.'

'What's group therapy like?'

'Mostly it's just sitting around with other quote-unquote survivors and we talk about our experiences, about adjusting to quote-unquote normal life.' Blair cracked her knuckles. Her fingernails were bitten down and the skin on her hands was dry and red. 'It's on Tuesday mornings in this church basement, and Mom waits upstairs and does crossword puzzles.'

'My oldest, Quinn, she loves crossword puzzles.'

'Oh, you have a daughter.'

'Two, actually. Quinn's thirteen and Josie is eleven.'

Sasha pulled out her phone and showed Blair photos of her family, and Blair seemed to be taken aback by the fact that Sasha had a husband and two daughters and that Josie and Quinn looked so much like her. But as Sasha swiped from photo to photo, she didn't feel the pride that she ordinarily did when she showed off her kids; instead, she felt strange and a little displaced, as though Blair were stuck in time and still sixteen while she herself had grown up and lived a life and had come back to tell Blair what it was like to be an adult. The unevenness of their respective lives felt unfair and even wrong, like a math problem that had been solved incorrectly. Sasha thought that she and Blair should have been on the same footing; weren't they both just a couple of girls still figuring out the world?

Blair elbowed Sasha.

'Hey. Guess what still works.'

She went into her closet and pulled out the star projector that she'd had since she was a girl, that Sasha remembered from sleepovers, both of them looking up at the ceiling and talking about the things that they could only talk about in the dark. Blair turned off the ceiling light and turned on the projector. It threw constellations onto the ceiling, and they listened to the motor of the projector whir and watched the stars slowly rotate around the darkened ceiling light.

'Didn't we count all these once?' Sasha asked.

'I think we thought we did.'

'I wish I could remember what number we ended up with.'

They fell silent and Sasha wondered if Blair was counting the stars on the ceiling or if she was doing what she herself was doing, which was replaying the events from twenty years ago in her head, trying to figure out how the two of them had gone from one thing to another. Sasha wanted to bring up what happened that night at the mall and tell her that it seemed so trivial all these years later.

'I think it's really cool that you haven't asked about it,' Blair said.

'Asked about what.'

'The Link — that's the name of the people in Vermont that I'd been living with.' She rolled over on her side to face Sasha. 'It's all anyone wants to talk about. No one ever asks about anything else that I did.'

'I want to hear about everything,' Sasha said. 'What if I stayed the night, like old times, and you can tell me whatever you want.'

Blair let Sasha borrow a pair of sweatpants and a faded t-shirt from a turkey trot on Cape Cod. Then she rolled out two sleeping bags on the floor and brought in a spare pillow from the linen closet. They got into their pajamas and settled into their sleeping bags and looked up at the stars on the ceiling and it felt like they were kids again.

'I'm sorry about everything that happened to you.'

'It happened to me as much as I happened to it.'

'What do you mean?'

'Do you know Newton's third law of motion? A lot of people think gravity is just some magnetic force coming from the core of the earth that attracts objects to it. When really, gravity's just the word we use to describe the attraction between any two masses. If I drop a balled-up sock to the ground, the force that draws the sock to the ground is equal to the force that draws the earth toward the sock.' Blair cleared her throat. 'Or this, right now, you and me, finding ourselves together again after all these years.'

'I like that.'

'I was studying astrophysics at Williams. This was, like, before everything.'

'Do you ever think about going back?'

'All the time.'

Sasha suggested that they see each other regularly, that maybe it was what both of them needed, and that maybe Blair could eventually meet Sasha's family. And while she told Blair more about Josie and Quinn and how they were doing in school and what their interests were and also about how Josie was, right now, going through the brand-new experience of being liked by a boy, Sasha yawned and felt her eyelids grow heavier and heavier, and she felt the sensation of sleep overcoming her, like a curtain being drawn around her mind.

In the morning, she woke up and saw that Blair was already awake and out of her sleeping bag. Sasha could see through the glow of the mini blinds that it was early dawn, which meant that out of habit she hadn't overslept at Blair's house and missed Quinn's soccer game. She rolled over and picked up her phone. There was a message from Grant, asking her if she could pick up bagels and coffee on her way to the game. And there were the usual amount of work emails on a Saturday morning, and she glanced at them to see if they needed her immediate attention. Like Grant's text, the emails could wait. Then she stretched and walked down the hall to use the bathroom, and this time when she washed her hands, she used one of the pristine bars of decorative seashell soap that she'd always been hesitant to use. When she walked out of the bathroom, she saw that Blair still wasn't in the bedroom. Sasha quietly roamed the house, hesitant to wake up Mike and Julia. But Blair wasn't in the living room or the den, nor the converted garage, nor the sun room. And then Sasha noticed that her car keys were missing, no longer sitting on Blair's bedside table next to where she'd left her phone overnight. And even though she knew that Blair was gone, along with Sasha's Outback, and probably halfway to Vermont by now, Sasha still rushed out the front door as though Blair would still be in the driveway, and Sasha could catch her, and join her.

P. KEARNEY BYRNE

46A to Dun Laoghaire

Lorna's place is basic, a room with bare floorboards in the top half of one of those tall houses in Dun Laoghaire that's sublet as flats. She shares with three others, two lads and a fat girl with skin problems. Lorna doesn't know them well but says they're grand. There's no door between their flat and the one downstairs and all the rooms lead onto a landing with an open staircase. To Annie, the place always seems crazy, everyone on the dole, people shouting up and down the stairwell, music blaring – Sex Pistols, Blondie, the b52s – the smell of fish and chips, the half brick that keeps the bathroom door closed.

Annie hasn't been home for almost a month now. She told her parents she was staying with her brother and his wife so she could study. They don't know about Lorna and they'll freak when they see her hair all gone. It was Lorna's idea to do the buzzcuts and Annie has a black scab on her ear where Lorna caught the skin with the clippers. They used wads of toilet tissue to stop the blood, squishing it down hard on the cut. For the next two days there were tiny sausages of bloody tissue behind Annie's ear and in her clothes, little balls of it caught in her underarm hair.

This evening, the two of them have walked the five and a bit miles from Dublin city centre and they're near the overpass outside the university. It's a fresh May evening, daylight still trickling across the treetops on the campus. The double-decker buses headed for town or Dun Laoghaire are nearly empty, cars infrequent and slow moving on the dual carriageway. Annie loves that she and Lorna are dressed the same. Levis, Doc Martens, and denim jackets buttoned tight. Lorna has a little knapsack stuffed with her essentials; a plastic bag of markers, rolls of stickers, and a penknife. They hit five pubs on the way out from the city centre, drank a glass of Guinness between them in each bar, shared a packet of salty peanuts and a glass of water, then did the toilets after. Lorna says it's her work in this life. Says she thinks for herself and this is her mission. Big changes are coming. Watch out. She's nineteen, a year older than Annie. She left school early, spent time in London in the squats. She's been to Greenham and says she'll go back soon. That's how she and

Annie met. At a meeting about the Womens' Peace Camp in D'olier Street. Annie only went along to see if there were any lesbians.

In the pubs, they've left a trail of graffiti, usually on the back of the door or at eye level on the wall beside the jacks. Mostly stickers in the Ladies, mauve-coloured women's symbols, or variations on it – a raised fist inside the circle, or two linked symbols – sometimes a word carved into a door. Lorna doesn't allow any messing about but in the Foggy Dew, for a joke, under *'Free Bobby Sands,'* she wrote *'With every box of Kelloggs Cornflakes.'* Though they both love Bernadette Devlin.

When they can get away with it, they do the Gents. Lorna is more daring, works faster. She'll dash in and leave her scars – that's what she calls them – in the cubicles, over the urinals, anywhere her marker pen can get a purchase. Drawings. A cock and balls with a scissors snipping the cock in half. Balls with a boot going towards them, or a dagger carved with her penknife. Words: *Prick. Bastard. Fancy having your dick cut off by a lesbian? Lesbians are everywhere. Watching you. You fuck.* Sometimes, after she starts writing, she can't stop. She drives the nub of the marker hard into the cement and paint of the walls. *Fuck you. Fuck you. Fuck you.*

Annie knows graffiti isn't her forte. If she hasn't thought it through in advance, she ends up starting letters. *Why does it matter to you that some women don't want you? There's plenty of straight women. Can't you see it's nothing to do with you?* Earlier, in the first pub, when she was writing, her face up close to the wall, the smell of men's piss heavy in the air, Lorna grabbed the marker from her.

'Get to the point,' she said, 'for fuck's sake.' She shoved Annie out of the way and scrawled on the mirror. *You bollix. Your girlfriend is a dyke. Fuck you.*

They'd had the usual hassles earlier in town. One piss head came over and sat beside them. *How are yiz girls, youse want a bit of company?* When they said they didn't, thanks, and asked him to leave, he got angry, called them names. *What are youse? Lezzies? Lesbos. Fucking cunts.* Another spat at Annie in McDaid's. She'd been nervous, jiggling her leg because he had a vibe about him and wouldn't leave them alone. He nodded at her fanny, asked her if she was nestling a Chinese egg in there. She told him to fuck off and he hoiked a gollier right in her face. A big glob that went into her eyes, ran down her cheeks and Lorna lost it. She stood up and pushed him off his stool, yelled at the barman to get this fucking psycho out of the bar. But the barman told *them* to get out, who did they think they were, assaulting his customers. Lorna called him a cowardly shit-head, a fucking hand-job, the barman yelled he was getting the guards, the filthy gob on her. When she kicked a stool over, he came out from behind the bar and ran them to the door, stood bellowing at them while they scarpered down Harry Street, laughing and shouting back at him.

They turned into Chatham Street and Lorna pulled Annie into a doorway, kissed her hard, using her strong little hips to pin her against the door. They were breathing fast, but still laughing, even with their mouths mashed together, teeth against teeth. Always after these episodes, especially after a narrow escape – dodging a queer bashing or a punch in the gob or throat – when they've got away, Lorna will drag Annie with her until she finds somewhere to shift her. Standing up, lying in the grass, in cubicles, up against walls and doors in back alleys.

Now, they're walking along by the bushes at the edge of the Belfield campus, a bit pissed from the glasses of Guinness and from not having eaten anything but peanuts all day. They're singing *Dance this Mess Around*. Before they get to the chorus, they stop, pretending they have mics, and yell out onto the road, *Why don't you dance with me, I'm not no Lim –burrrr -guhur*, and they scream with laughing. A car goes by, pumps the horn at them, and they shout after it, giving it the finger. They're a bit quieter after that, walking closer and closer until they stop, pressed tight into each other. Lorna pulls Annie into the bushes at the edge of the path. She slides her hands inside Annie's clothes, finds her way to skin.

'Cold fingers,' Annie says through a mouthful of tongue.

'Shut-the-fuck-up,' Lorna says. 'Shut-the-fuck-up and let me at you.' She pushes Annie backwards through the dogwood and gorse until they reach a birch stand. She shoves a hand down the front of the Annie's jeans until she's in her knickers. She grins.

'Yeah,' she says, working her fingers. 'Thought so. You dirty fuck.'

Annie doesn't know if she likes this kind of sex-talk. Her body likes it though.

After they've finished, they fix their clothes and emerge onto a pathway. They can see the blocky grey buildings of the university.

'Which one's yours?' Lorna says. She's never been on the campus, says it doesn't interest her, pile of wank. So Annie doesn't talk about it anymore.

'You can't see it from here,' she says.

Since she met Lorna, Annie's been missing lectures. When she told Lorna her subjects were English, Psychology and Philosophy, Lorna asked who the philosophers were? Who the psychologists were? All men, right? Fuck-all women, right? Another pile of men making shit up for more men.

Lorna's got it sussed. It is a pile of absolute wank. Except for some of the novels, maybe. Annie's decided to not sit her exams. She told Lorna in an offhand way, like it was no big deal, and Lorna shrugged, said, yeah, why waste her time on that shite anyway, and went on eating her Rice Krispies.

Annie's parents will go mental when they find out. She'll have to repeat the year.

Lorna has started walking toward the buildings. 'This hole needs some livening up,' she says. 'Let's see what we can do about that.'

'No,' Annie says. 'I don't want to go in there.'

'You mean you don't want me to go in there?'

'No, just… Please let's not go in there.'

But Lorna is already skipping ahead, turning to walk backwards every now and then, grinning and making faces. 'Time for me to see what this shit is all about,' she calls back. 'The Big Secret.'

In the arts block, the concourse feels hollow and smells of rubber. Lorna is still ahead of Annie, a small figure in the wide corridor, twirling and whooping, her hands in her pockets, her hands in the air, laughing and calling out, a strange echo to it. *Okay, I see it all… okay… here we go… the corridors of power.* She looks all around, runs her fingers along the brickwork walls, examines the floor plans and diagrams, sniffs at the bins. Annie trails behind her, tries to keep her head down and watch out at the same time. Some of her friends from school are doing First Year Arts. Normally, they'd all eat together, go across to the bar after lectures. If Paula and Siobhan saw her now? Her long hair gone, the sex stuff scrawled on her arms in biro, the things Lorna might yell at them. But the arts block is almost empty. Just one or two older students mooching about. Annie lies down on a wooden bench outside one of the lecture theatres and thinks about what Lorna said to her in bed the previous night; that she was a great fuck, that she was beautiful, that she's never known anyone like her. And suddenly, she's not scared anymore. Her stomach has relaxed and her throat isn't so tight. Who cares anyway? Who cares what anyone else says about her?

Lorna is still roving about, whistling, humming, slapping her hands together every now and then. Annie takes a Wrigley's from her denim jacket, peels off the foil, and stuffs the gum into her mouth. It's a bit old and crumbly, but the peppermint is strong. There's a whoosh of sound as Lorna sits on the bench and slides up close to her. She taps her fingertips lightly on Annie's forehead, touches her eyebrows, her eyelids, forcing them closed for a couple of seconds.

'Yeah,' she says. 'We need to fuck this place up a bit.' She stands up again, takes a roll of stickers from her knapsack, leans across Annie and starts making a pattern on the wall with the stickers. A women's symbol. Underneath, she writes in black marker. *Dykes exist. You ignorant fucks.* She underlines *fucks* three times then goes to the heavy double door of the lecture theatre and peers in through the glass.

'This where you get your lessons?' she says. Annie sits up.

'Lectures. Yeah. Sometimes.' Lorna pushes the door open and disappears inside.

'Come on, Annie-fanny,' she shouts. 'Gimme the grand tour.'

By the time Annie gets inside, Lorna is already far below at the front of the auditorium, waving up at her from behind the big brown desk. Annie follows her and the further down she goes, the weirder it gets, making her dizzy. She's only ever sat in the top three rows at the back, near the entry doors. The steps are wide and she has to land with two feet on each one. When she reaches the bottom and stands behind the podium looking up, she gets a shock. It's the reverse of what it's like from the back row. From up there, the lecturer always seems miles away, a tiny gesticulating insect. But from down here, everything seems close, you can see right up to the back, could see the expression on every face.

At Annie's feet, Lorna is squatting down fiddling with plugs and sockets, trying the locked cabinet doors under the desk.

'What you looking for?'

'The mic.'

When she can't find it, Lorna straightens, puts her hands flat on the desk and springs easily onto it, her boots clumping on the wooden surface. She raises her arms, palms upwards and shouts at the top of her voice, '*Hey* shitheads! Listen to *me*.' Even without a mic, her voice flies high, filling the auditorium. She laughs down at Annie.

'Fucking hell,' she says. 'Imagine everyone trapped in here, listening to what I have to say. Jaysus!' She laughs again, scoffs. 'Some hope of that. These fuckers have it so easy. Same old, same old.'

She looks around with her eyes narrowed, left and right, up to the seats at the back, down to those at the front. She makes a disgusted, huffing sound. With her hands on her hips, she strides to and fro on the desk, printing the varnish with the soles of her Doc Martens. She stops in the middle, faces the rows of empty seats. Looking up at her, Annie sees how her tidy bum clenches in her Levis as she steadies herself. There's a few seconds thrilling silence, then using her full lung capacity and leaning slightly back, Lorna's voice fills the theatre.

47

'Here's something your books won't tell you,' she shouts. 'Cos we're *not in* your books. You know nothing about us, you *fucks,* in your cosy little lives. Because you can't fucking see us.' With her head thrown back, her legs spread wide, she looks amazing, like a bantam fighter, and Annie's heart beats faster. She has a weird urge to scramble up beside Lorna and hump her leg like a dog, then trample all over the desk, laughing and yelling and stomping her feet.

Above her, Lorna lifts her right arm and flicks her hand so her finger points at the room, roving in a semi-circle. 'But *we* can see *you*. We see what you do. We know how you think –'

There's a sound from high up at the back of the lecture theatre. Annie jolts when she spots a security guard making his way down the steps.

'Hey! What are youse doing in here?'

Lorna stops speaking, watches him for a few seconds, a sneer on her face.

'Hey ya Big Bollix!' she roars. 'In your Big Uniform.'

'Youse don't belong in here.' He's still moving down toward them, a clumsy step-by-step rocking. 'Get out. You've no business. You're trespassing.'

Lorna stands for a moment, staring at him. Then she jumps from the desk and she and Annie run up the other aisle toward the door, their Docs squeaking on the steps. The security guard changes tack, makes his way horizontally along a row of seats, aiming to intercept them. He's slow-moving, like a big ship. Annie knows he doesn't really want to catch them and they get away easily, jogging along the concourse. She laughs, expecting Lorna to do the same, maybe do a few of her trademark whirls and shouts. But Lorna doesn't do any of that, and Annie goes quiet too.

Outside, it's dusk. From the campus treetops, the birds flute their last calls of the day. Annie walks alongside Lorna beneath the long concrete shelter that leads to the college restaurant. It's always Lorna who makes the pronouncements after these things and she's waiting for Lorna to speak. But Lorna says nothing, her hands shoved into her jean's pockets, shoulders hunched, head slightly averted so Annie can't see her expression.

They turn toward the exit to the dual carriageway, crossing the tarmac in front of the restaurant. As they pass Belfield bar, Annie stops and points.

'See that pre-fab building? That's the student bar. If you want, we could go in. Fuck it up a bit?'

Lorna turns her mouth down, lifts and drops her shoulders.

'What's the point?' she says. 'What fucken difference does it make?'

'But isn't that what -'

'Fuck off,' Lorna says. 'What would you know?' and she keeps walking.

From the overpass, Annie spots a bus coming from town. Probably the 46A to Dun Laoghaire.

'You think we should run for it?' she says.

Lorna doesn't answer, just sprints away and Annie follows. She's faster than Lorna usually but, this evening, she can't catch up. Lorna gets to the bus stop before the bus pulls in, sticks her arm out. She jumps onto the platform, but keeps waving one arm, swinging from the pole at the door, so the driver can't shut it. When Annie gets there, panting, Lorna grabs her hand and yanks her onto the step.

'See,' she says to the driver as he gives them their tickets, 'That wasn't too hard, was it?' He shakes his head, rolling his eyes, looks into his side view mirror, and pulls out on the road.

There are a few people sitting downstairs, looking out the windows in the yellow light. Lorna and Annie head upstairs, holding the rails and lurching as the bus swerves. The top deck is empty, and they take a seat close to the front. Lorna sits by the window and looks out. Annie can see part of Lorna's reflection in the glass, her eyes turned down to the road.

'You okay?' she says. Lorna turns. Her expression is odd.

'Yeah,' she says. 'Grand. Tired is all.' She turns away again.

Annie watches her for a few seconds, her high, sharp cheekbone, the small curve of her ear, the way her blonde hair, because it's shaved so tight, looks fresh and new. She's still following the lines of her profile when Lorna twists in her seat, looks directly at her. She puts one arm around Annie's shoulder and with her other hand, brings Annie's face near. She closes her eyes and kisses her. It's a strange kiss, her lips soft and warm. She hasn't shoved her tongue into Annie's mouth, and she hasn't immediately started running her hands up under her tee-shirt to grab her breasts, pinch her nipples. Annie opens her eyes and sees Lorna looking at her. They smile at each other and Lorna kisses her again. They begin to hold each other tighter with an intensity that's very different from their usual lust. Annie is a bit scared at what it means, the feelings it brings up in her, and the surge of sexual feeling has a hot seam of something strange running through it. The bus pulls into a stop, moves out again. When Annie opens her eyes again, Lorna's face is tipped up, her eyelids closed and fluttering lightly. She looks younger, delicate and vulnerable, and a tendril of disgust unfurls inside Annie. She shuts her eyes and shoves her tongue into Lorna's mouth, puts her hand between her legs and forces them apart, feels the power in doing that, and Lorna begins to move over her hand in a way that's slightly painful, crushing her fingers. As Annie brings one knee onto the bus seat, so that she's above Lorna, there are clattering sounds behind them followed by a man's voice.

'Evening, girls,' the voice says as the man slides into the seat in front of them. He sits sideways, leaning against the window, his arm along the chrome bar at the back of the seat. Annie and Lorna move apart, stare at him. He's maybe thirty with a thin face and he smells of Guinness.

'Get a load of youse two,' he says and he winks at them. 'Don't let me interrupt. Get back to what yiz were at.' He points to his crotch. 'Yours truly at your service. For when yiz need the real thing, like.'

'Why don't you fuck right off, you wanker,' Lorna says. She's lowered her head. Her top lip is raised on one side, displaying her eye-tooth.

Annie looks around. The top deck is completely empty except for the three of them.

'Lorna, don't.' She tugs at Lorna's arm and begins to get up from her seat. 'Come on. Let's go.'

The man takes out a cigarette and lights it, blows smoke into the air.

'Take it easy, girls,' he says. 'Just being friendly. I mean, yiz are obviously looking for a bit of company. Doing it on a public bus and all.'

'You stupid prick,' Lorna says. She has her teeth bared. 'You haven't a fucking clue what you're dealing with.' The man starts laughing, a low wheeze, half coughing through his smoke. He keeps his cigarette dangling from his lips.

'Oh, I know what I'm dealing with alright,' he says. 'Keep your hair on.' He looks deliberately at Lorna's shaved head. 'Oh, right,' he laughs to himself. 'Too late for that.'

'Fuck you!' Lorna rises a few inches and, holding the chrome bar with one hand, she leans over the back of the seat and punches him straight in the mouth with the other. Even though it's her left hand, her fist smashes the cigarette into his face, sparks go everywhere, and he jumps up shouting, *Jesus Christ, Jesus Christ*, holding his mouth. He scrabbles out of his seat, rubbing ash off his shirt, pushes past Annie who's half-standing in the aisle, and makes a grab for Lorna.

'You mad fucking cunt,' he says. 'What the fuck did you do that for? Me lips is burnt.'

Lorna's in a crouch on the bus seat and they whack at each other, yelling. From behind, Annie yanks at the man's bomber jacket, but can't get a good grip. Lorna has her penknife out and tries to stab him in the arm. When he sees the knife, the man backs off yelling, 'Jesus Christ, get off me! You fucken mental or what?' Annie has a hold on the end of his jacket and she wrenches at it. The bus starts pulling in at a bus stop. The three of them sway and the man breaks free, heads for the stairs. Lorna jumps into the aisle, snatches at him and misses, but as he goes down the stairwell, she swings one leg back and kicks him right up his arse. He doesn't say anything, there's just the sound of him banging down the stairs, battering off the sides.

Annie and Lorna stand in the aisle, panting and saying, 'Fuck,' over and over. There are loud voices from downstairs. The bus stops, then pulls out onto the road again, and a kid of about seven comes up the stairwell with his mother. The woman looks at Annie, then at Lorna, takes the child's hand and pulls him back down the stairs. Lorna gets in between the seats and peers out at the path below. When she leans a hand on the window, the blade of the penknife clangs against the glass.

'Yeah,' she says, laughing to herself. 'Look at him running off. Stupid little bollix. Run off home to your mammy, you little prick.'

She's still laughing, her cheeks flushed, when she turns back to Annie. She comes close to her, pushes her into the seat and makes her slide up against the window. She bends over the chrome bar and digs the blade of her penknife into the seat cover where the man was sitting. She tugs upwards, grunting, and the plastic rips open, small bits of orange sponge catching in the blade. She closes the knife, slides it into her jeans pocket and pulls Annie's head close to her face.

'That'll fucken teach them,' she says, the words muffling into Annie's mouth. 'That'll show them who they're messing with.'

JOHNNY EUGSTER

The Truth About The Lies People Told About Cattle

1. JAPAN FISHERIES BOARD – YUTO YAMAMOTO

'Leaving aside, for one moment, the direct assault on a member of our fishing fleet, you've got to admit, it's brilliant,' says Yuto Yamamoto, the chairman of Japan Fisheries Board, leaning back in his plush, leather chair at the head of the boardroom table. 'It's got consumers buying beef but when they are eating more beef, they are eating less fish. We need a gimmick of our own.' He rises to his feet and slams a copy of tabloid newspaper *Yukan Fuji* down on the table with the headline *Cow sinks boat, Bullshit declares insurer* clearly visible. His impeccable double-breasted suit pulls smooth by its own weight, as he walks to the thirty third floor window overlooking Tokyo Bay. He stands, pensive, searching the water below for answers. He sees, in the glass, wave lines furrow his forehead and behind him, the board members, sitting, waiting, deferential, for him to provide the solution.

'The advertising agency will now present.' He runs his right hand through his silver hair and turns, nods at a young man in a blue suit, standing by the door, who opens it to let them in.

Their cover slide declares: FIGHTING FOR FISH, Japan Fisheries Board, 15th September 1995. Yuto sits, impassive, through their presentation. It is marketing-speak, a language he dislikes, all pretension and aspiration: hot air.

'Stop,' he says finally, cracking his plaster-cast stare, a hint of joyful surprise in his eyes. 'Please go back one slide.'

Kimi Hirashita, the advertising account director, an attractive thirty five year old with long, black, bouncy hair and, appropriately, a slightly protruding fish-like face, relaxes her posture just slightly. 'Hai, Yamamoto-san,' she says, with a formal clip, pressing the remote. 'Our third concept, Aquarium Office Building, is our recommendation.'

On the projection screen is an ordinary drab-looking, ten-storey office block in a city somewhere in Japan. It is presented as an aquarium, full of a wide variety of ocean-dwelling fish: schools of sardine, tuna, salmon, jellyfish, squid, swordfish, sting ray, octopus, dolphin to some types of shark. The water fills the building and the fish can be seen clearly through the windows.

Kimi flips to the next slide: a graphic depiction shows the timeline progress of the water filling the structure, floor by floor.

'We weld-seal the building as we fill it using a nearby fire hydrant. We cut the power and leave one hundred kilos of sea salt in the lobby. The toughened glass will withstand the pressure and we estimate a fill time of thirty six hours, possibly less.'

She flips again. Fish tanks on stands of different heights are displayed. 'We think it's important to showcase the entire menu of seafood to remind consumers of the wide choice available. We anticipate extensive media coverage, which, of course, we will instigate, anonymously, ourselves.'

She flips again, to show a close up of the front door, leading through to the ground floor reception. A sign hangs above it: 日本牛肉協会 Japan Beef Board. Yuto smiles; she may as well be presenting a washing detergent or a soft drink, for her composure betrays no concern about promoting an illegal act of wanton destruction to property. Takeru Kobayashi, his counterpart at Beef, will have a shock when he gets to work next Monday morning. He chuckles out loud.

2. MITSUBAN MARINE – HIRO HONDO

'Mitsuban Marine is one of the largest insurers in Japan,' Hiro Hondo tells the group of teens, dressed smart in their school uniforms, gathered around him in reception on the tenth floor of Mitsuban Tower in Sapporo's Central Business District, eager to begin their week long summer internships. 'Marine offers insurance on anyone and anything connected with the seas.' He has been selected to nanny them because he is young himself and can make insurance seem sekushī (sexy). 'At the hotto shotto (hot shot) end of Marine is space capsule retrieval, oilrigs, tsunami beacons, sub-marine, navy, and super-yachts. At the jānīman (journeyman) end is some guy that wants to go for a dip at the beach.' There is giggling from the girls and knowing nods from the boys. 'Please fill out your employment papers and help yourself to refreshments. Your mentors will be here shortly.' As Hiro returns to his desk he wonders where he fits in. Fishing Boats, once you get into blue water vessels, are certainly not tens on a picking up girls in a whisky bar scale but sixes or sevens maybe? His direction of travel is, therefore, hotto shotto, for he is in his late twenties and ambitious with it, but this trajectory, he thinks, is now in question. He collects a blue file from his cubicle; he bends to check his hair in the mirror hanging from the partition. He looks at his reflection: handsome with slightly prominent cheekbones. He lingers, hoping the mirror will make sense of the nonsensical situation. Don't be a hero, Hiro.

'How do I look?' He turns to his colleague, Nakamura-san, a middle-aged salary man, who sits in the opposite cubicle from him.

Nakamura swivels in his chair, nods, 'Normal, Hondo-san, very normal.' He smiles, for he means it as a compliment.

Hiro passes the next cubicle.

Ito-san rises from his seat and looks at him, already knowing the question. 'Yes, most definitely very normal, Hondo-san.' He too nods approvingly.

All his colleagues appear at the open side of their rabbit hutches, as he calls them, bowing their heads slightly as he passes, acknowledging his valour, as if he is a samurai away to a battle that can't be won.

He is in no-man's land now, beyond the safety of Fishing Vessels and into Ferries and Tug Boats. He is just about to enter Container Vessels when he feels a tugging at his sleeve.

'Hiro, don't do it,' says Misako Kondo, the only woman in Fishing Boats, who has rushed after him on impulse. 'I know the company tagline is *Expect the Unexpected*, but that's bullshit, they hate the unexpected, so they will hate you. And this is worse than unexpected, it's unexplained.' She lets go of his sleeve, because she is attracting the unwanted attention of colleagues from Container Vessels, who peer round the edges and over the top of their cubicles, always rather too happy to see her.

'Thank you, Misako.' He reaches out and touches her arm. 'I have repeated the predicament to Captain Sato and he will not revise his application form and, if I'm honest, I believe him.'

'Then you too may sink like his fishing boat,' she says, lowering her sparkling eyes, aware that puddles are welling in the recesses.

'This is the course I am on.' He turns from her and continues on his way.

3. ANTONOV AN-124 'CONDOR' HEAVY-LIFT TRANSPORT AIRCRAFT – KAPITAN ANDREI SOKOLOV

Returning to Moscow empty is a waste, so when some extra cash presents itself: well, such are the times, the Soviet Union is over; these days everyone looks out for themselves. Make what you can of it, thinks Andrei Sokolov. It is a bad idea from the start. The loading at Dolinsk-Sokol, a cold, military airport on Russia's windswept Sakhalin islands, just north of Japan, is chaotic: the noise of the turbofans and the refuelling fumes are alarming; the cattle are on edge. Once on board, with the ramp closed, there is a calm among them, for a while. But consider, for a moment, the dynamics of aircraft and flight: after landing, take off is the most vulnerable stage; balance is key. All payloads, without exception, be it troops or a couple of T-90 battle tanks, are weight assessed, positioned accordingly and secured. Try explaining that to a herd of cattle.

They are clear for take off. The four D-18T turbofan engines are deafening. As they pick up speed down the runway, the engines whine and so do the cattle. The more nervous they get, the more they shit; the more they shit, the more methane fills the hold. Even a small spark could do it, but, as it turns out, this is not the gravest risk.

The Antanov hits optimum speed, inclines and takes off. This is when the problems begin. The good news is the herd is well within payload capabilities, equal to about half a T-90 tank. The bad news is they are stampeding around the hold.

'Our best hope is settling them once we level,' Sokolov tells Maxim Kuznetsov, his co-pilot.

'Oh sure, then we serve an in-flight meal and put a movie on.' Kuznetsov, is red in the face and shaking.

'We deplete the oxygen supply, make them sleep.'

'That might work. If we get to that altitude.' The Antanov see-saws violently from the internal turbulence. Suddenly a bullock is up there with them, on the flight deck.

'Do me a favour?' Sokolov calmly asks, glancing sideways, 'Get rid of it.'

Kuznetsov, startled, releases his harness, dumps his headset, jumps up and forces the bullock, by its head, back out through the door.

It whines at the herd, perhaps telling them what it has seen through the cockpit window that, believe it or not, they are fucking well flying. Somehow it has scaled the flight deck ladder and this is the way Kuznetsov, with the help of the crew, pushes it back down again. The fear from the cockpit bullock spreads: flying? No one said anything about flying. Protest moos add to the panic moos. They stampede along the hold towards the tail.

'Kapitan, they've made a hole in the fuselage, we can't take much more of this,' Popov, one of the crewmen, yells into the cockpit.

Sokolov looks down at The Sea of Japan, shimmering blue, sparkling in the sun, 10,000 feet below them. 'Okay, get them out.' He looks across at Kuznetsov, and shrugs *win some, lose some* with his shoulders.

'Crew, return to your seats and buckle up,' Sokolov commands.

Kuznetzov flicks some switches on the console to his right. 'Deploy oxygen masks. Opening cargo door.'

Sokolov looks over at him. Years flying sorties against the Mujahideen together, dropping thousands of tonnes of munitions, causing untold numbers of fatalities had never before brought forth his co-pilots moon-shaped eyes.

'Expedite climb.' Sokolov pulls the throttle back, brings the nose up, losing the horizon.

Their hooves skitter on the floor grills as they fail to grip against the angle of ascent. The cattle bellow.

'Goodbye Rolex Oyster,' Popov says over the radio.

'Goodbye Gucci loafers.' That's Volkov.

'It's not meant to be whores of Grachevka.' And Kozlov.

There is laughter. Sokolov looks sideways. His co-pilot peers out of the window, away from him.

'Kuznetzov?'

Kuznetzov turns to him, his eyes red and streaming. 'Hey diddle diddle, the cat and the fiddle, the cow jumps over the moon,' he says into his mask.

'What is that? English?' Sokolov asks.

'A nursery rhyme my daughter sings.'

4. WAKKANAI CHUO ELEMENTARY SCHOOL – RIKU SATO

When invited to bring a picture for *what do your parents do day*, Riku Sato, aged six, a pupil at Wakkanai Chuo Elementary School, in Wakkanai, the capital of Sōya Subprefecture, in the north of Hokkaido, knew exactly what to draw.

With every reject, he makes a big show, to his mother, of tearing it up with a stamp of the feet and declaring: 'It's not good enough, I'm starting again.' On the fourth draft, he is finally satisfied. Such is Riku's pride, after all his hard work, as he prepares, in his classroom, to withdraw the page of acrylic paper from his satchel.

Sasaki-san, standing up on the teacher's platform in her neatly bunned hair and pretty blue dress, thanks his desk mate, Aki Yoneyama, who smiles shyly, and returns to her seat next to him.

'Riku, would you like to bring your picture up, to show the class?' Sasaki-san smiles politely at him.

'Good luck,' Aki whispers as she sits down on the bench seat next to him.

'Hai, Sasaki-san,' he replies. He withdraws the picture, keeping the subject matter hidden, and walks, jauntily, up to the platform. He feels his face warming. He remembers his father's words: *A fisherman has nothing to fear but Godzilla rising from the sea and Godzilla is make-believe, so then, there is nothing at all to fear.*

'Now then, what is this?' Sasaki-san tries to fathom his picture. 'Would you tell us about your picture please, Riku? And hold it up so everyone can see.'

'Hai, Sasaki-san,' he replies, turning to face the class. He hesitates, but sees Aki smiling up at him, so he bravely holds it up in his left hand, while pointing at it with his right. 'My father is a fisherman and this is his boat.' The boat is drawn in brown crayon with a wheel-house in red, rigging and nets in green. 'He catches mackerel and scallops mostly, but one day, he caught a cow.' The cow, up above the boat, is black with yellow spots, with speed lines trailing it, to show that it is falling, at speed, from the sky. His father is drawn, oversized, on the deck of the boat, in a bright yellow oilskin waving a big net directly under the plummeting cow as if it is any normal day's fishing out on the Sea of Japan. 'The cow crashed into his boat and made a big hole.'

Some of his classmates gasp as the picture hooks their attention.

'And then what happened, Riku?' a girl asks.

'And then the sea came into my father's boat and it sank, mostly.'

'And what happened to your father, Riku?' a boy asks.

'He clung to the broken boat, until he was saved.'

'Sasaki-san,' asks a girl at the front, her hand in the air. 'Can cows really fly?'

'In Riku's picture, they can, but in real life, no,' she says, patting Riku nicely on the head.

'But in real life, this one could,' Riku insists, his eyes wide and his head nodding, hoping Sasaki-san will yield on this important exception. It is these words that return to torment him, later that afternoon. It starts with one boy, running circles around him, with arms extended either side, like the wings of a plane, but instead of an engine noise he moos.

And then a clever girl, knowing, somehow, too much of everything, calls out: 'Hey Riku, look, I'm a Cowasaki,' as she launches herself, arms spread wide, off the grassy bank on the far side of the playground. For they have indeed learned cow in English class and she has attached it to a well-known maker of airplanes.

As everyone laughs, Aki sits down next to him on the bench, picks up his crumpled picture, from where he has dropped it on the ground, and flattens it back out across her knee. 'I believe you, but maybe, if you'd drawn the cow in black and white, and not yellow, they would too?'

5. WAKKANAI CITY POLICE STATION – DR MAYUMI KIMURA

The basement cell is not nearly as forbidding as those that appear on police crime dramas. There is a dark blue carpet, purple curtains, a flat-screen TV on the wall, a thermostat, a chest of drawers, a table and two chairs, a small en-suite bathroom and a single, well-made bed that has been tidied for her visit. It more closely resembles a hotel room, albeit a cheap one. Perhaps, she thinks, he deserves better, for his crime, if falsifying an insurance claim can be called that, has become a cause célèbre.

Captain Haruki Sato, a stocky, handsome man of thirty-eight and two months (for she has gone over his file) with a chiselled face and square jawline who wouldn't look out of place on a police crime drama, rises politely from the table, nods and offers, with his outstretched right hand, the other seat to her.

'Good morning, Captain Sato, I am Doctor Kimura.' She places her files down on the table, removes her jacket, hangs it on the chair back, then pulls her skirt smooth before touching down gently on the curved Formica seat.

'Hai, good morning, Doctor Kimura.' He follows her lead, sits back down and places his craggy hands back on the table in front of him and folds them, with just a slight air of resignation, she thinks.

'I am a designated psychiatrist qualified by the Mental Health and Welfare Law to conduct psychiatric assessments in relation to legal procedures, such as yours.' She raises her right hand to her head, and with her slender fingers, combs back her long black hair which has fallen across her face during the sitting. 'I am appointed by the sub-prefecture court to give expert testimony for your case, is that clear?'

His fingers, interlaced within his folded hands, flutter slightly, she notices, as if they are wings contemplating flight.

'Hai.' He nods, curtly, with a just perceptible roll of the eyeballs and patient intake of breath.

First she takes him through the preliminaries: confirming his identity, age, personal history and so forth.

'Now, I will show you some images. Please tell me what you observe.'

She places four images on the table: dragonfly, seagull, cow, paraglider. 'Now does any one image stand out for you?'

'The third image, cow,' he says.

'Why?' she asks, raising her voice, slightly, as if expecting a different answer.

He hesitates, clenching his jaw. 'The cow cannot fly.'

'Thank you, Captain. Now please apply yourself to these next four and tell me what you observe.' She swaps the images for: iceberg, cow, submarine, whale.

His jaw is rigid like stone and she thinks she hears his teeth grinding.

'Cow, again,' he says.

'And why cow again, please?'

'The cow does not belong in the sea.'

'Good, but there is another reason that I have grouped these images together. Can you guess what it is?'

The way that he twists his neck, which could be tiredness but is more likely frustration, makes her think he knows.

'Iceberg, submarine and whale have all, upon occasion, been responsible for the intentional or unintentional sinking of fishing boats,' she says, perhaps a little too smugly, 'but never before has anyone claimed to have been sunk by a cow.'

'I have read the headlines: *Livestock make Laughing Stock of Fishermen* and yet why would I lie? Do they imagine I would sink my own boat, so far from land, putting my entire crew at risk, to claim the insurance? That I find more unbelievable.'

6. SEA OF JAPAN – CAPTAIN HARUKI SATO

There is solitude in the sea. It is distant and dangerous and there are rarely witnesses to what happens out here. These are the thoughts swimming around his brain as he clings to the foredeck of his fibre-glass scallop boat or what's left of it. The aft deck and engine tore off and are out of sight now, on the bottom already, thinks Captain Haruki Sato, an experienced scallop skipper in his late thirties. This is fortunate because the weight would have dragged the whole boat down.

'I just prayed to Ebitsu, so we'll be rescued soon,' says Sato, wearing his yellow oilskin under an orange life-jacket that is inflated around his neck and chest.

'How fast do you think it was going, Oyakata?' asks apprentice fisherman, Nobu Mori, a skinny young man of twenty-seven, his clothes drenched and his body shivering.

Sato smiles. Even now, as they cling to the wreck counting down the last minutes of their lives, Nobu uses the honorific title *Oyakata* (master) when *shit for brains* would suffice. If he had acted sooner: revved the engine, moved the boat a few metres forward, it would have missed them. 'That's a good question, Nobu,' he replies. 'I would guess a cow to be similar in weight to a small car, say 750 kilos.'

The waves are picking up and the hull of the boat is not coping well. It is in danger of keeling over, pitching them back into the cold water again. The maths is a welcome distraction.

'How far would you say the cow fell? Anyone?' Sato puts the question to the six man crew who, mercifully, are all uninjured and clinging to the hull with him.

'10,000 feet, Oyakata?' replies Nobu.

'Good, so we know height and mass,' Sato gets the class engaged, 'how do we determine speed at impact?' Now that he has them thinking about something other than their impending deaths, he reflects on how he is going to explain this to the authorities. When you see a cow in a field and hear it mooing, it raises no questions, but when you are out at sea beyond the sight of land and hear mooing above you at some distance and closing, it raises many. At first, you don't think cow, for how could it be? Is it a tornado brewing up suddenly or an ocean vortex sucking air down through its swirling core? Is there a malfunction aboard? Could the sonar be alerting us to some undersea obstacle? Such is the Captain's checklist. Anything might be possible, but not what happened next.

The first cow to strike the surface was about a kilometre away, followed closely by others until the trail of impacts came closer and closer. It was only about five seconds between understanding that there was a cow on a collision course with their vessel and throwing themselves overboard. The cow, travelling at…

'Therefore we need to find the square root of velocity squared that is 200,000,' says Aoto Watanbe, the other apprentice fisherman, aged twenty four, whose eyes move up and down in their sockets as if rummaging in his head for the answer. 'That would be 450 k.p.h., say.'

There is a round of one-handed applause as the crew slap their free hands against the hull, although, it turns out, this is a bad idea. The hull turns over throwing everyone back into the water....the cow, travelling at 450 k.p.h., exploded on impact, but, to its credit, mooing until the end, and split the boat in two.

7. FLYING COW BURGER BAR – AKARI ANDŌ

Ever since Sumo Burger opened its franchise nearby in the Kita Ward of Sapporo, the capital city of Hokkaido Prefecture, Akari Andō's Bunny Burger Bar has paid the price. Everything about Sumo is sumo: the size of the burgers, the size of the restaurant and, she whispers, not so quietly, to her remaining loyal customers, the size of the bill. But what seems to make the difference, is not the quality of the meat nor the service, no, she can beat them on both, it is the marketing they use.

Outside, in their parking lot, no matter what the weather, two sumo wrestle inside a circular, sandy pit that is itself shaped like a giant burger. One bread bap at the base, another to make a roof above them, so that they themselves are representative of the fat, juicy meat that customers can expect to find within.

'It's not an arse I'd choose to sink my teeth into,' says Akari, the owner of Bunny Burger, who inspects her make-up in a small compact mirror and flutters her long eyelashes, as if better arses are meant for her.

'No, but they are smart arses and you could learn from them, Akari,' replies her best girlfriend, Miko Ono, crossing one leg sideways over the other on her bar stool, so that she can lean in closer over the Bunny bar to drink her glass of white wine. 'Look at this.' She slides a folded copy of Hokkaidō Shimbun over the counter to Akari, standing behind the bar in her clip-on bunny ears, wiping some imaginary mess from the slate surface.

'What am I looking at? The Aum Shinrikyo sarin gas attack?'

Miko retrieves the newspaper. 'No, sorry, other side, here.' She flips the paper and points at another article: *Flying Cow Sinks Fishing Vessel? And Pigs Might Fly.*

And that's how Bunny Burger became Flying Cow Burger; for the widely reported, tall tales of Captain Sato and his crew were a lot more on brand than Bunny Burger could ever hope to be. Students from, perhaps ironically, the nearby University of Health Sciences were lured with the enticing prospect of free meals to market the rebrand.

'Look, it's perfectly safe, you'll be fine, you're tied on, just jump will you?' Akari hisses into her walkie-talkie to a student dressed in a black and white cow costume and wearing a pair of wings who is perched on a platform protruding from the roof of the three storey building and attached by a bungee chord to a scaffold above. 'Oo mai goddo, I should have hired Captain Sato instead,' she says, aside to Miko, who giggles into her hand.

Finally, the student jumps and, despite a successful trial run, crashes heavily into the flimsy trestle table, breaking it in two. The prize, a platter piled high with a pyramid of Flying Cow Burgers, cushions his fall. He is then returned to the air by the retracting chord, his face covered in mashed burger and ketchup, the sight of which resembles multiple injuries causing gasps from the crowd and flashes from the assembled photographers.

'So clever, like the cow crashing into the deck of Sato's boat. Art imitating life.' Miko raises her voice while looking sideways at Akari.

She is dumbstruck by the collision and her shipwreck of a launch ceremony.

Miko claps and even the dangling cow, soiled with burgers and ketchup, bouncing up and down, spreads its arms and moos, so that the disaster appears deliberate.

Miko lifts Akari's hand, triumphantly, into the air, turning her round towards the crowd. 'The Artist, ladies and gentlemen. Truly inspiring.'

8. GERMAN EMBASSY, MOSCOW – DR SUZANNA SCHILLING

For staff stationed in embassies around the world, such as Dr Suzanna Schilling, there is a hardship grading which determines salary and benefits. London or Paris, for example, are so popular that she would almost pay to go there; war-torn or poverty-stricken countries, on the other hand, she would almost pay not to. Moscow is neither the most popular nor the least; she is, therefore ambivalent about her posting as the resident defence attaché at the German Embassy.

Tall and attractive at thirty-eight with muted ginger hair, she is a welcome and glamorous addition to the diplomatic circuit, which mainly revolves around events and briefings at other embassies and The Ministries of Defence and Foreign Affairs of the Russian Federation. Her main issue with the circuit is the drinking: it makes her say things she shouldn't. *Just turn it down*, her husband tells her, but to do that is to be disrespectful, so she drinks and saves face.

'Defence Attaché Schilling,' says Victor Kublenkin, the Deputy Director of Russian Air Force Command, walking into the crowded, wood-panelled state-room where all the Embassy functions are held, 'a pleasure to see you again.' He extends his dark blue, uniformed arm, takes her hand in his and, she thinks, makes a point, as usual, of squeezing slightly too hard.

A waiter, in a pressed white jacket, appears by their side, presenting a silver tray of filled champagne flutes and vodka shot glasses.

'When in Rome.' Schilling takes two shots and offers one to him.

'We Romans, we love our vodka,' replies Kublenkin, taking the glass.

After she has drunk three, the chatter in the room resembles snippets of radio broadcast briefly heard when flipping through radio frequencies.

Kublenkin breathes into her ear. 'Tell me something, Doctor Schilling, a state secret, perhaps?' he asks, smiling politely but with a glint of mischief in his eye, wanting something he can report back with.

'Three holy sisters are talking,' she begins, feeling a little hot in her olive green dress uniform, 'the first sister says, "I was cleaning the priest's room and do you know what I found?"' she pauses, '"Some pornographic magazines—"'

As soon as he hears *pornographic*, Kublenkin interrupts.

'One moment, Doctor.' He taps a uniformed shoulder with three gold stars attached to blue epaulette, in a group behind them. Within seconds, they have an audience: diplomats, military brass, ambassadors. 'Yes please, Doctor, again.'

So, she starts over.'" —What did you do?" the other holy sisters ask. "I threw them out." The second sister says, "Well, I was putting away some laundry in his room, and I found some condoms!" "Oh my!" gasp the others. "What did you do?" they ask. "I poked holes in them!" she replies. The third sister faints.'

Those who speak English explode. She has to pat Kublenkin's back because she is worried he will choke or have heart failure, he is going so red. He recovers and translates the joke bringing forth yet more laughter.

'You know, for a diplomat, you are funny, Doctor Schilling. These sisters—' he stops to catch his breath again, '—so much better than a state secret.'

The crowd around them disperses and Kublenkin leans in closer 'And I have something for you, Doctor, a bad joke. It's about cows that fly. Perhaps you are the person to tell?'

He hands her a folded copy of Moscow tabloid, *Komsomolskaya Pravda* and points at a headline: *Cow sinks fishing boat. What a load of old bullocks, says insurer.* So he tells her of the misadventures and subsequent disciplinary actions of Kapitan Andrei Sokolov. How he is the Kapitan rightly behind bars and Sato the one wrongly. Perhaps she might have a discreet word with her colleagues in Tokyo? It's all a rather unfortunate and embarrassing mistake.

'So, you see, Doctor Schilling, in the end it is I who tell you a state secret,' says Kublenkin.

And so it is that Captain Sato's story that both begins and ends with an act of God, is finally confirmed and he and his crew are released.

PETER ADAMSON

I need you to be Harold

It was a day that began in innocence. A hard, cold, blue New England sky, a weekend without commitments, a straight-from-the-oven bagel and the leaf colour at its scarce-believable best as I crossed the river and picked up Mass Pike heading east out of Boston.

Ever since I had first seen the photos, I had been drawn to small-town New England. Don't ask me how you can be nostalgic about somewhere you've never been, but there was no denying my soul-tug towards those white clapboard houses glimpsed through sycamore trees or arranged around village greens and watched over by modest Congregational spires. And so after settling into my year's teaching appointment, I had taken the first opportunity – a Thanksgiving weekend – to rent a car and head for the Berkshires.

That first day was all I had expected of it. But rather than following my itinerary, I will check my story straight into the Red Lion Inn, Stockbridge, where I had reserved a room for three nights. These New England coaching inns – open fires and polished floorboards, rocking-chair porches and herb-scented gift shops – are all part of my iconography and the Red Lion, which first opened its doors at the close of the French and Indian Wars, did not disappoint. My single room was on the third floor and its parchment lampshades and hand-quilted bedspreads were all I had imagined. I stowed my overnight bag in the wardrobe and sat on the edge of the bed, savouring that moment of anonymity that all hotel rooms offer; that moment of reluctance to claim bare surfaces and take possession of empty drawers, that moment that whispers seductively – 'you could be anyone'.

I had not eaten since Bagels-R-Us but didn't fancy a table for one in the main dining room where families and friends were already arriving for Thanksgiving dinner. Instead, I took a stool in The Widow Bingham's Tavern, picked up the bar menu and ordered the 'Famous Red Lion Bloody Mary'. My surroundings – low-ceilinged, oak-panelled, lamp-lit, with ketchup bottles on check tablecloths and antique kitchen paraphernalia strung from the rafters – fitted perfectly into my idea of the weekend.

Perhaps it would be better to preface what happened next by acknowledging something about my state of mind at the time. I had spent the day,

64

as intended, pootling around quiet villages and stepping inside achingly simple white churches with box pews and clear-glass windows. Unlike de Tocqueville (the subject of my first teaching semester), my attraction to such places was almost entirely unexamined, a vague yearning without much thought as to what I might be yearning for. Perhaps on that account, as well as the Bloody Mary on an empty stomach, I soon began to sense an undertow of dissatisfaction. Was it perhaps the sense of having been only a spectator, my face pressed up against the window of a world in which I seemed to have invested some unarticulated hope? Or was it to do with what I imagined those New England villages to represent: a world of more stable norms and values, of community and belonging, a world that could still be understood? I should perhaps also mention that, even at the best of times, I am given to this kind of half-think.

A long pull at the icy furnace of the Famous Red Lion Bloody Mary jolted me back to The Widow Bingham's Tavern, now rapidly emptying itself into the dining room. It was just after half past seven and soon the only ones left at the bar were myself and a woman of about my own age who, when not looking at her watch, was twisting round to check the lobby for arrivals. Embarrassed as I am to confess to it, the words that came to mind were 'Bergdorf-Goodman'. The one friend I had made on the faculty, though progressive in all the usual campus ways, had a habit of classifying the women of his acquaintance by a department-store metric. If I have it right, this entirely subjective scale ranged from Walmart and Macys through Bloomingdales and Saks and finally to that rarity among women, a Bergdorf-Goodman. In case it comes up again, I had better also mention that such problematic ways of thinking have a tendency to surface in unguarded moments and have to be quickly slapped down in a kind of woke whack-a-mole. On this occasion, I paid penance by ordering a second Bloody Mary and devoting my attention to the bar menu.

I had decided on the Red Lion's Famous Hand-Carved Turkey Sandwich with sage stuffing and cranberry mayo and was hesitating over whether to start with a cup of New England clam chowder when my weekend took its bizarre turn.

'English, right?'

I had only spoken two words in her hearing, but it had obviously been enough.

We talked about the Berkshires for a while, and I think I might have gone on a bit too much about my feeling for New England domestic architecture because her attention kept straying towards the reception desk out in the lobby. Eventually, with another glance at her watch, she asked for her tab. I stood to help her with her coat, a camel-coloured cashmere that I imagined might have cost more than my entire wardrobe. Smiling a speechless thank you, she picked up her purse from the bar and walked out through the lobby into the night.

Alone now, apart from the barman who was checking optics, I drifted off again on that same current of something unfulfilled. Could it perhaps be a sense of not really belonging, of lacking an authentic identity of my own, some place to stand? Through the bay window of the Widow Bingham's Tavern, I saw the indicator lights of a car flash once as the doors were unlocked.

'Get you something to eat, sir?'

I was on the point of ordering the turkey sandwich with a side order of fries when there was a swirl of the camel coat and Bergdorf-Goodman reappeared on the barstool next to me.

'Sorry, but could I just ask you something?'

'Sure,' I said, wondering why I suddenly seemed to be performing a bad impression of Brad Pitt.

She took the menu from my hand and placed it back in its stand, dismissing the barman with a smile. 'I was thinking, if you're about to dine on your own this evening, how does a traditional Thanksgiving dinner in one of those lovely old New England homes sound?'

Faced with nothing more than a dumb look, she proceeded to unburden herself of a narrative about a new boyfriend who was supposed to be driving up from New York to be taken to meet her family for Thanksgiving and who ought to have been here an hour and a half ago. 'Rather obviously,' she concluded, 'he's a no-show.'

'So... you're asking me instead?'

Floored by this scintillating repartee, she placed both hands on the bar rail.

'Look, this is the thing right here. There is no way I can go back and say I've been stood up. No-oo way. It's too long a story but... way back... I guess I made up a serious boyfriend.' She paused to let this sink in. 'Like lots of girls do that?' she said, as if she had been accused of something. 'Anyway, thing is, I over-elaborated and got found out. Ever since, my Mom and sisters and all, well... you get the picture? There were "looks" when I said I was bringing Harold home for Thanksgiving.'

The barman, perhaps aware of a small drama being played out, was polishing glasses and pretending not to listen.

'You mean you'd like me to... stand in for this Harold?

She tossed a fall of soft, shining hair back from her face.

'It's just that when I heard you speak it just seemed like serendipity... you know? Harold's a Brit, too.'

I also took a glance at the reception desk in the lobby. 'Well, it's very nice of you to ask me.'

'Does that mean you'll come?'

'Would I... I mean... would I have to impersonate him?'

'No. Well, yes, I guess. In a way. But it's okay. No one knows a damn thing about him. Expecting me to show up with a Brit in tow is all.'

'You mean I could just... be myself?'

* * *

Outside in the street, she took my arm. 'This is so-ooo good of you.'

My rental car was the first in the lot and I already had the keys in hand. 'So, I just follow you?'

'Why don't we take mine?'

'Then you'd have to drive me back.'

'No problem. The thing is' – she glanced at my compact Chevvy Malibu with the bent Massachusetts license plate – 'I think I might have mentioned that Harold drives a Porsche coupé.'

Her perfume hung between us in the cabin of the SUV as she drove us out of town, heading west on Old Main. 'I'm Candice by the way, Candice Eliot. Don't tell me your name. I need you to be Harold. You cool with that?'

I had the sensation of wading out to sea and being about to lose the sand between my toes, but we were already turning onto a broad avenue lined with Greek Revival and Federal Era homes discreetly hidden among the trees.

I struggled to engage my brain. 'Isn't there anything I should probably know?'

'You're divorced and you work on Wall Street is all.'

We were turning again now onto a gravel drive winding through tree-shadowed lawns.

'Great,' I said, 'I don't know anything about finance.'

'Just stay wa-aaay off the subject. Pop loathes bankers anyway.'

Between the rhododendrons, I saw that we were approaching a well-lit Federal Era mansion.

'Maybe I should know how we're supposed to have met?'

'Motivational training course in the city. Don't elaborate.'

'You work on Wall Street too?'

'No, I was running the course. I'm a psychologist.'

* * *

67

The entrance hall was all sconces and chandeliers as the stranger I had become shook hands and smiled through a blur of Thanksgiving wishes and half-heard introductions. Supper had obviously been delayed and I had the inspired notion of apologising to Candice's mother for my late arrival. 'Oh, we expected it,' she said graciously, 'I95 is a pig anywhere near Thanksgiving.' And then we were ushered into a candle-lit dining room reeking of furniture polish and old money. To my relief, I was seated between Candice and her nephew, who must have been about ten and who solemnly shook hands and introduced himself as Aldus Franklyn. The scene was splendid: leaf and flower arrangements in fall colours glowed on the oak of the refectory table; pewter chargers gleamed dully amid the sparkle of cut-glass goblets; fat beeswax candles made bright halos making it difficult to see the faces opposite, half-hidden in any case by the vegetation and a line of swing-lidded tureens.

Unwrapping a warm roll from a cotton napkin, it occurred to me that gastronomic curiosity might see me through the first few minutes and was soon being informed that the sprouts were dressed with maple and walnut, the stuffing studded with chorizo sausage, the parsnips glazed with cider and honey, with a choice of caramelised sweet potato or mash with buttermilk. Once or twice I failed to respond to people who began with 'So, Harold, tell me…' but the general noise level, amid all the carving and the passing of plates and pourings of wine, offered blessed cover.

When dessert was eventually brought out – marshmallow pumpkin pie with walnut crust – I struck up a conversation with the nephew, who had so far made no effort to conceal his boredom. When I asked if he found adult conversation a little dull, he suspended his spoon and delivered himself of the opinion that it wasn't really conversation at all because everyone kept interrupting and so no one got to finish what they were saying and so none of it made any sense and it always ended with everybody laughing at something that wasn't even funny.

Coffee was taken in the drawing-room – log fire, plaid armchairs, Hepplewhite-Sheraton style antiques, Audubon prints on the walls – where the conversation continued to be much as young Aldus had characterised it and was too disjointed to pose much of a threat to an impostor.

Towards the end of the evening, Candice's mother stopped by the two wing-back chairs in which Candice and I had been facing each other, half-hidden. 'And where might you two be planning on going tomorrow?'

The idea of tomorrow seemed oddly alien in the situation but at least the question offered me safe ground and I stuck to my actual itinerary: 'I'd been rather hoping to see Hancock Shaker Village, Mrs Eliot.'

'Isabel, please. Oh yes, you must see Hancock. Don't miss the Great Barn. And there's Edith Wharton's place of course, just up the road. But you must be dreadfully tired after that beastly drive. Your room's all ready, so you two just go on up whenever you want. There'll be plenty of time to talk tomorrow.'

Candice grimaced an appeal for me to play along and reached for my hand. 'Yes, I'm quite tired too. I think we'll go on up.'

* * *

Still holding my hand, Candice closed the bedroom door behind her.

'Oh my god, was that just amazingly awful?'

'No, but...' I gave a trapped look around the room and its centrepiece – the enormous mahogany, paisley-quilted sleigh-bed on which a dozen cushions had been scattered with careful abandon. She grinned and was about to say something when her cellphone rang: like the world interrupting, or an alarm clock breaking into a dream.

'Darling, what happened? Where are you?'

She gave one of her apologetic grimaces and disappeared into the bathroom, closing the door behind her.

The bedroom décor should have been calming: beige wallpaper with a faint silver stripe, rag-work rugs on mellow old floorboards. I crossed to the window seat. Outside, what I had at first taken to be a small balcony turned out to be the platform of a fire escape from which white-painted ironwork zig-zagged down into the darkness.

I tried the sash and felt an initial give. Directly below, another gravel drive headed out across unlit lawns. As far as I could tell, Candice seemed to be doing all the talking.

It was almost a quarter of an hour before she emerged.

'That was Harold. He's been stuck on I95 for two and a half hours with no signal.'

'You told him what happened?'

'Laid the whole thing right on him. He's cool with you. He'll be here in twenty minutes.'

'He's coming here?'

She raised both hands and made a calming gesture.

'Okay, we have ourselves a situation. Now, here's what happens.'

She tossed the fall of hair back from her face in the manner that was becoming familiar.

'He takes the long-cut and comes in off Glendale. Brings him in right here under the window. I told him not to slam doors. He comes up the fire escape' – she took a step towards the window – 'says how-d'ya do and all, and tosses you his keys. You shoot down the fire escape and take off. Hang a right on Glendale and a left when you hit 20. Five minutes and you're tucked up at the Lion. In the morning, it was all a dream.'

'But... what about you – tomorrow, I mean? You just... tell everyone the truth?'

'Exactly what Harold said. But that's not what's going to happen. No way can I go down and 'fess up. I told you before, I have form.'

'But you can't just go down to breakfast...'

'With a different guy? That's exactly what I can do. Ever hear of change blindness?'

Dumb had become my default expression.

'Dan Levin? Kent State? Come on, it's about as famous as the one where the guy in the gorilla suit walks across the court in the middle of the game and no one notices.'

At this point, I found something in me starting to push back. 'Candice, I haven't the faintest idea what you're talking about.'

She sat down on the end of the bed. 'OK, get this, right? Unsuspecting sophomore gets stopped on campus by some guy asking the way to the library. While they're talking, two other guys carrying a door come between them. When they've gotten by, the guy asking directions has changed places with one of the guys carrying the door. The subject doesn't even notice, just carries on explaining the way to the library. Change blindness. Got it?'

'You mean you're just going to go downstairs tomorrow morning with a different guy and no one's supposed to notice?'

'God, you sound exactly like Harold. I know it sounds weird. Everyone thinks *they* wouldn't be fooled. But trust me, it'll work. Some other campus someplace, they offered a bunch of students five bucks to be in some dumb psychology experiment. When they trot off to sign up, the clerk at the desk disappears to get the consent forms. Comes back, he's someone else. Do they notice? They do not. 'Real-world change detection paradigm', Daniel T Levin and somebody, 2002 or thereabouts. I know Dan. Smart guy.'

'But, I mean, I was down there for a couple of hours tonight...'

'Doesn't signify. Look, I don't have time right now to teach the whole semester, but here's the four-one-one: retaining visual data so as to be able to reproduce it later is not a strong point of the species. There's a bunch of names for it – inattention blindness, encoding failure, representation failure – but the take-home is you have to be paying a whole lot of conscious attention if you're planning on retaining any specifics over time.'

70

I started to shake my head but she tossed her hair back again and waved the doubts away.

'Fact is, Harold – what's your real name by the way?'

'I'm Paul.'

'Well, fact is, Paul, you need to encode data if you're going to retrieve it. And all those folks tonight, in the middle of all that "have some more pumpkin pie and no I shouldn't really and okay maybe just a small piece", let me tell you, no one was doing a whole lot of encoding. Data you take in like that just isn't retained because it's not organised. Retrieve and compare? Forget it. Makes you think about the justice system, doesn't it?'

But I wasn't thinking about the justice system. I was listening to a voice telling me I'd been given an out and should take it.

Candice looked at her watch. 'Harold was the same, circling the airport for an age before touch-down. But, believe me, it'll be fine. We'll go down in the morning – beautiful day, did you sleep well, yes thanks very well, try the blueberry muffins – and no one will say a damn thing. Even if they think something's not quite kosher, they'll think it's them – their confusion, their hangover, their memory for faces. And everybody else will just be carrying on like nothing's different, so we get the bandwagon effect going for us as well.'

'But, I mean, does this Harold even look like me?'

'Doesn't signify. God, the guys who swapped places at Kent State were a whole lot different. You and Harold, not so much. But I'm telling you, it's not what people saw tonight that matters. It's what they can pull back in tomorrow morning. What they encoded. And given that you haven't got two heads I can tell you right now the encoding number they did on you – male, white, British, college-educated, acceptably middle class, period.'

I looked down from the window to the disbelieving lawns.

'Well, if you think it could work...'

* * *

Harold performed an exaggerated impression of a burglar climbing in from the fire escape. He grinned, shook my hand, said 'Hi, how was my dinner? and then hugged Candice, swaying her from side to side while rolling his eyes at me over her shoulder.

'So, I just need to get this straight,' he said, releasing her and brushing a few flakes of fire-escape paint from his jeans. 'The master plan is, I go downstairs in the morning and pretend to be someone who was pretending to be me tonight?'

I smiled back nervously. 'You think it might work?'

'Can't see it myself,' he said cheerfully, 'but Candy "trust-me-I'm-a-psychologist" seems to think it'll be okay.'

'Of course it will,' she said, 'and don't call me Candy.'

She came over to take my hand. 'Tell me your name again?'

'Paul. Paul Morley... I think.'

She smiled and placed both hands lightly on the tops of my shoulders. 'Well, thank you, Paul Morley, for being my knight in shining armour. You were so-ooo great tonight.'

'No problem. But, look, do you think you could, you know, ring me or something to let me know what happens? It's just that I'd be curious to know...'

'If we get away with it,' said Harold, still grinning.

'Sure,' said Candice, 'I'll call you.' She punched my number into her phone while Harold forced the window up another couple of inches.

'I'll go then,' I said, hoping I could manage Harold's way of stepping elegantly over the sill.

'You'll need this – careful not to spit gravel.' He was handing me the key fob, emblazoned with the famous Porsche red, black and gold crest. 'It'll be okay in the lot for a couple of days. Just leave the key at the front desk. I'll pick her up Sunday.'

From the foot of the fire escape, I gave a wave to Candice and Harold, silhouetted against the light of the bedroom window, their arms around each other's waists. And then I was driving tentatively through the night, listening to the slow crunch of gravel and wondering how the perfect innocence of my New England day was ending in the bucket seat of a $300,000 Porsche 911S having just left the bedroom of a Bergdorf-Goodman by the fire escape.

* * *

She did not call until the evening.

I had slept long, breakfasted well and, despite the cold, taken coffee in a steamer chair out on the porch where a notice offered guests packed lunches and 'curated New England experiences'.

Hancock Shaker Village may be a museum, the ghost of a community strangled by its own strictness, but it did the job of bringing me closer to whatever grail it was that I was searching for. Those quiet, whitewashed rooms, the timelessly crafted furniture, the patient spinning wheels and looms, the worn and sculpted shovels, the delicacy of copper-riveted boxes – all of it pierced me as nothing else had done. It spoke of an aesthetic liberated by restraint and was as moving to me as whole galleries of fine art.

Glad to have my mind differently stocked, I skipped lunch and headed east toward Historic Deerfield. A long drive in the country, I have found, works like a gimbal, allowing the mind's quivering compass to align itself with the field of underlying concern. And so it proved as I was passing Bryant State Forest on that Friday afternoon. The Shakers of Hancock Village were more than a tourist curiosity: they had known community and belonging and purpose in full measure, and it was a knowledge reflected in all that they did and made and owned and used. Not even for one evening would it have been easy for them to assume any other identity. Nor, I speculated, would they have failed to devote their full attention to what was before them.

By early afternoon, I was visiting the first of the homes on Historic Deerfield's Old Main Street. It was as rich an afternoon as I have ever passed, and as close to time travel as it gets. But more important than the signs marking the years outside each of the houses along that tree-lined village street was the journey along that poignant continuum from brutish survival to a gentler, more refined existence: lap-jointed log homes became mud-caulked, then shingled, then weatherboarded, then finished in a lime of crushed-clam shells or built in stone or ballast brick; batten-and-plank doors with strap-and-pintle hinges acquired panels, transoms, sidelights, porticos, while interiors that had been plastered with mud and dung became limed, whitewashed, and eventually lined with duck-egg blue wainscoting and floral wallpaper; open three-stone fires gained hearths and chimney breasts, oak lintels, carved wooden mantels and, later still, marble surrounds. To walk the length of that street was to walk through a history that was not about the strut of politicians and monarchs but the struggle of families and communities to leave behind the primitive, to win for themselves a measure of comfort and refinement. I felt their struggle in everything I saw and was moved by their silent presence.

* * *

The traffic was light for a Friday evening and I was free to settle down with my thoughts on the hour-and-a-half drive back to Stockbridge. I still had not heard from Candice. And when she came to mind now, as I took the road running parallel to the river, even her name seemed to have come from a world and time more distant than Historic Deerfield.

Somewhere near Conway Hills, I stopped to take on coffee in a roadside general store and found myself in a wooden labyrinth of aisles that wandered between grocery mart, barbershop, hardware store, haberdashery, apothecary, stationer, dairy and ice-cream parlour. When I found the counter, I helped myself to coffee from a jug and carried it out to the stoop where half a dozen chairs were arranged around barrels.

As a pair of motorhomes passed in a sedate convoy, I checked my phone and reflected on the past twenty-four hours. It was easy enough to see Candice's home – with its chandeliers and gilded mirrors, its excess of foods and wines, its streams of information and entertainment accessed from leather recliner chairs – as just a continuation of the centuries-long journey I had followed at Deerfield. Easy, too, to lament what had been lost along the way – something that was perhaps too far gone to see clearly but which might still inspire a longing. Maybe it was the loss of an intelligible connection with the workings of things, or perhaps it was the thread of belonging spun too fine, the identity attenuated, the seeing and the experiencing gradually becoming less conscious, life less encoded, as the pace of the undreamt-of had quickened to a blur.

I looked out across the highway. Set back from the road behind deep lawns was a Greek Revival home whose columns would have been more to scale on the Parthenon. Only when concluding that what had been lost was the nobility of the struggle did I remind myself of what had also been left behind: lives cut short by illness or blighted by boredom and bigotry and the cruel censoriousness of closed minds. I stood to go back into the store to help myself to a refill. Over the door, a hand-painted sign announced 'If we ain't got it, you don't need it'.

I had just returned the thermos to the counter when my phone sounded out the opening bars of 'Sweet Baby James'.

'Hi, how's it goin'?'

'Candice, what happened?' I walked back out onto the stoop.

'Nothing is what happened, like I said. Harold was cool, just hung in there and assumed they all knew who he was.'

'I can't believe it.'

'Yeah, only one who wasn't blindsided was the nerdy nephew. The one you were talking to?'

'Aldus? He knew?'

'Shuffled right up alongside after breakfast. Asked me out of the corner of his mouth – "what happened to the guy you were with last night?"'

'What did you say?'

'I told him there was a ten-spot in it if he kept schtum. He's saving for an astronomical telescope.'

'But, I mean, with your folks, it was okay?'

'Fine, like I said. We took off first thing to see that Norman Rockwell picture. You know the one? "Freedom from Want"? We're just having leftovers tonight, by the way. Harold was great. Pop offered him a cigar. Anyway, thanks again for saving my ass. I'll call you if I get to Cambridge, right?'

'Sure,' I said, 'that'd be great.'

I wrapped my hands around the K-Cups coffee. So it was true. Harold had taken my place, as I had taken his, and the switch had not been noticed. Except by Aldus, who thought all adults absurd. Or at least no one had noticed enough to break ranks. Candice had been right about the encoding, and about what it amounted to. Probably any reasonably well-spoken, white, college-educated Brit with some loose change in cultural capital would have done.

It was getting dark and I had miles to go. I took a sip of the still-scalding coffee. Did I feel used, anonymised? Or had it been a relief to be cut loose, freed by not being known? Without a community of expectation, it had been quite easy to imagine a different self, a self based not on anything that might be within but only on the expectations of others. Anything resembling a real me had shrivelled within the chrysalis of my pretence. Later, when I had time to reflect, I realised to my shame that the most disturbing thing about the experience was not its strangeness but its familiarity. I slipped the phone into my jeans pocket. One more whole day of unmoored anonymity still lay before me; one more day when I could be anyone.

I left the last of the coffee and reached to pick up the key fob with the famous red, black and gold crest.

ABI CURTIS

Pollinate

The air vibrates with the slow rumble of the earth. I think it's about a 3.5 or maybe a 3.8. It's warm today. The flowers tremble on their stems. One or two apples, not quite ripe, fall as the vibrations subside. A few of us look up at each other. I carry on working, barely missing a beat, touching the plants to my arms, my wrists, the creases of my elbows. I'm lucky to have this job, and I don't mind the work. I want to look dedicated. I know that I'm doing something important. There are only a few jobs someone inexperienced can do to get a passport, to be allowed to cross borders. I want to go backpacking after I graduate from uni, and I didn't want to work in a weather factory, or plucking chickens, or sorting virt-coins. This way, I get to be in the fresh air, and I can listen to music on my chip or headphones. I'll admit, I was a bit scared about the gene activation. This is the only student job where you need a procedure. But it was a doddle, barely a scratch. Just a slight sting.

So, now I'm a trainee pollinator for the summer. I probably won't take it much further, make a career out of it, but it's a start, something for the CV. And I can go to Europe after. Ride the train, visit Venice, Berlin, Dublin. I'll have a bit of money and a pass. I can't wait.

After the tremor, Dominic says, - Woah, hold on to your hats! and grins at me. The dark hairs on his arms are glistening with golden powder. I like Dom; he's cute and a bit cheeky, thoughtful too. But there isn't much point in getting attached to anyone here. We'll go our separate ways soon enough. Besides, I can see he likes Briony. She's his type: all violet hair and willowy limbs. She lost her footing last week in a tremor of 4.1, which is not like her, and she's got a red graze all up her arm, but it only adds to her vulnerable appeal. She works quickly, more practiced than the rest of us; this is her third summer. She wants to get enough money together for a flight to Asia, and she's driven. She wears just a vest and tiny shorts, even when the weather is cool, to maximise her pollination areas. She moves amongst the foliage in this incredible dance, big headphones over her ears. She presents the backs of her knees, her elbows, her arms, the nape of her neck, behind her ears, her bare ankles, to pollinate everything around her. She thrums and flows meditatively, eyes half-closed, skinny limbs dusted with light, like she's at a silent rave.

76

It's beautiful to watch. I don't even try to copy her. I'd look ridiculous, and the gene-activation takes time to get you to this level as a pollinator. She dances all day, reaching up to apple blossoms while her legs brush poppies, bluebell and campion.

There are seventy acres of multi-culture here – a mixture of fruit trees, wildflowers and crops, and about twelve of us per acre. There is a dark woodland nearby where we aren't allowed to go. Sometimes I long for the cool shadows I imagine there. But they like to be able to see us at all times. I watch the slow deepening and blooming of the clouds and love the rain to come down from time to time so we can have a break. Briony shivers in the rain, but I don't think she likes to stop working either. When she has to take a break, she stuffs down more food than you can imagine for such a waif, and it's always something sweet. Pancakes with apple sauce are her favourite, and she'll drink massive mugs of tea with spoonfuls of sugar. I guess the way she works, she burns it all off.

We sleep in a bunk barn. I was surprised there is no gender segregation. I guess because about eighty percent of us are girls; it doesn't make sense to give the boys special treatment. Our Overseer is pretty cheap anyway. They want to get the most profit they can from their workers and still pay well enough to attract them. When there's no sun for a few days (which is quite often when the smog storms come) we have cold showers. It's ironic that the solar showers work best on hot, clear days when you'd prefer a cold shower. The Overseer is okay though. She's a squat, strong looking woman who wears bright lipstick and big aviator shades like she should be flying a plane. She walks about, mostly silently, her and her deputies, checking up on us. She's always covered up, neck to toe, with long sleeves and high collars, white, heavy gloves, everything tucked in, like she doesn't want to get any pollen on her, or she's worried about the sun. Which seems odd. I asked Dominic and Briony about it early on, and they just smiled as if they knew something they shouldn't.

- Is she allergic or something?

Briony smirked. – Or something, she said. And I could see I wasn't going to get any more out of her. It was like when I asked her for tips about her movements, her pollinating dance. She was lying on her bunk, reading a book, her violet hair fanned out on the hemp pillow. Dominic looked up to listen to the response too.

- I dunno, she said. I wasn't always able to do it so easily. My first summer I just used my wrists. They got really sore and red, so I started using my elbows for a break.

She leafed the pages of her book as she spoke, and frowned.

- Then I just tried, like, my neck. It sorta felt nice.

At this, I caught a half-smile from Dominic. Perhaps he planned to use that insight.

- By the end of the summer I was moving differently, and, I suppose, it's practice. The following summer I felt more attuned. And now. Now it's easy. Like riding a bike. Like swimming. Like...

Sex, I thought. I know Dom thought it too. She opened her book back up and ignored us the rest of the night. I don't think she really knows how she does it, how it works. That's why it's so elegant.

As for me, I try to emulate her approach, if not her style, exploring different parts of my body to see where the pollen might be attracted, where it might stick or drift. It's quite an art to get it to float and shiver on the fine hairs of your skin, and then to coax it away again onto the next flower. You take and give; give and take. You never keep it for long. It's borrowed light.

Part of the job is spent in the classroom, attending training sessions about how all this used to happen by accident, quite easily, how the honey bees and bumble bees would settle into the cups of the flowers, loading pollen into their holsters like old-time cowboys. Promiscuous as porn-stars, all got up in their gold and black velvet, seeing a purple world through their screen-like eyes. When the Overseer shows us pictures, Briony stares at them with her mouth half-open, like they are the most beautiful things she has ever seen. We watch slides of honeycombs, architectural and dripping, and I swear I see her wiping saliva from the edges of her lips. Personally, I'm not so sure about the bees; they look like little monsters to me. When the Overseer showed us a film of a hive, the humming was so intense and stifling I almost felt they had got into my ears and were burrowing into my brain. My skin prickled all over.

- Bees evolved very nicely alongside the flowers they pollinated, with some flowers only being pollinated by one specific type of bee. Now we have only one half of the partnership, and we act as substitutes.

- Like a failed romance, piped up Dominic.

- It is a crisis, the Overseer shot back, lowering her aviators for a second. It has been a crisis since long before any of you were born.

But I secretly thought: I wouldn't have this job without the crisis. I have never seen a real bee. And that was a strange, selfish thought I suppose.

As the summer goes on, I get into pollinating. I think it is becoming more natural to me. We each dance with our own music plugged in, but sometimes I swear I can pick up the rhythm of Briony's playlist, or Dominic's, or one of the others, watching them move in the waist-high crops. A few birds scatter up as we make progress across the fields, then they wheel away into the woods. I wonder often about the woods. They glow violet in the fading light as the sun goes down. The pollinators are silhouettes, like shadow puppets on the wall of the sky, bending, reaching and dipping, humming their tunes.

At night, the bunk barn grows warm with our bodies. More pollinators, even greener than I, are shipped in during late summer because the crops are not on track to yield enough. We have more training and more classes. I dream about stamens, petals, apples bruising and going rotten on the grass. I fantasise about Asia, but then remember I want to go to Europe, and wonder has Briony been talking about her trip? I ask her to tell me her plans, and as she does, I recognise what she says.

- Have you told me this before? I ask one night, yawning in my bunk.
- No Amber, this is the first time you asked me.
- But the yoga thing, and the stuff about Thailand?
- Nope, only just told you.

She's right – she doesn't brag about these things. She's quiet unless you ask. But I have these distinct images in my mind about it. I see the green of the Andaman sea; the pale beach; great rocks covered in lush grass poking out of the water. These images are a cross between a memory and a photo from a brochure.

- It's going to be amazing, though, says Briony, her eyes closing ready for sleep. Doing yoga on the beach, swimming every day, hiking. You know?

And I do know, somehow. At least I think I do.

Today, another tremor. I think this one was a 4.3 maybe. I stumbled and fell over, but partly because I was practising lifting one leg up to brush my knee against the corn. A thrill of fear went through me, as if I was in more danger than I actually was. At lunch, Dominic sits down with a bowl of rice and vegetables.

- Did you hear about Debs? She got really hurt today – one of the apple trees fell in the tremor. Must have been on its way out. Crushed her leg.
- No, I say, I didn't realise. A crawling sensation flashes up my shin and then subsides. I've never been good hearing about injuries.

Dom chomps on his food. I'm eating a piece of carrot cake, a rare treat because we've all done well this week and the crops are improving. But it tastes savoury somehow, as if it's been chopped with a knife used on onions. I swallow and drop the rest in the bin. Dom raises his eyebrows; wasting food is frowned upon. I ignore him and walk back to the fields. I'm on a break, so I don't do anything, but pollen collects and drifts from my skin anyhow. I peer over to the woods, and amble towards them. They shimmer in the hot afternoon.

I don't see why we can't go into them. Perhaps the Overseer doesn't want us idle. But it is still my break, and I don't feel like eating anymore; there's a strange taste in my mouth. I step to the edge of the field where the crops peter out and the wild flowers stretch their blue and red flames. The pollen drifts towards the fine hairs on my legs – filings to a magnet. I feel the coolness of the trees, see the brown shadows through the brambles that delineate the wood. Blackberries cluster their dark knuckles. There's a coppery, ripe smell, a sweetness I can taste. The air is edible. As I breathe, I hear a sudden rush of voices as though I've opened a door on a party.

- Amber.

The Overseer has never addressed me directly before. I turn. What are you doing here? She lowers her aviators, almost theatrically.

- Ah, I was on my break. Just…Just hot.

I know I shouldn't be here, and try to appear naïve.

- Don't stray from the acreage, she says, and walks quickly away. In the distance I see Briony and Dominic have stopped and are looking at me.

We learn about beehives in class, and drones in particular. The spoiled, cosseted boys, bigger than the rest, fed, fattened and loved. Until they had done their duty, fertilising the queen, then were killed, a necessary sacrifice for the good of the hive. The screen in the classroom flickers with hexagons and the segmented bodies of bees crawling and creeping over one another.

I'm not sleeping so well now the bunk barn is almost full. I don't know if it's the heat, or just the sense of all those extra bodies around me under the corrugated roof, but my dreams are unsettled. Briony has moved to the bunk next to Dom's, opposite mine. I jealously watch her fall asleep within minutes each night. I can see her chest moving rhythmically as her breathing settles, and the mounds of her breasts in the half-light. Maybe this is why I'm dreaming about her in particular. Guilty dreams. I wake aroused.

My pollinating is improving. I listen to my playlist, my musical tastes becoming more eclectic as others recommend tunes. I like rock for the flowers, classical for crops. I stretch my body towards the blossoms, anther to stigma. The continued practice is paying off. In breaks, when I'm drying the sweat from my skin, I glance towards the woods, but I don't go close. I can't get away with that again. One lunchtime, when I'm eating a bowl of QuornPlus, with sugar sprinkled over it, one of the new pollinators approaches me. I'm not sure if they're a boy or a girl, with their short hair and square-jawed, moon-shaped face. They say their name is Georgie, which doesn't help.

- Hi, how long have you been here? Georgie asks, no preamble.

- I guess six weeks or so, I say, sounding irritated, like someone who knows how things are run so well they can't be bothered to explain. I don't like the way I sound.

- I wondered, how do you move like that, when you pollinate? What's the trick?

I take a bite out of my sugared Quorn and chew slowly while I consider.

- I practice. I'm at this all day, we are, all of us. All day. I watch Briony

- I gesture to where Briony spins among the apple trees - She's the best at it.

Georgie follows my gaze and frowns. - I think you're better, she (or he) says simply. So much faster. More elegant.

At this, I stop as if someone has snatched a breath from me, and my skin shudders at the abruptness, scattering pollen. Tears burn in my head. I'm jealous, mad. But I'm not sure with whom, or why. Georgie wanders off to find food, oblivious to my emotions. I see that in the orchard Briony is crouching down as if a tremor had just passed, but the world is still.

- Why can't we go into the wood? I whisper to Dom before nightfall. He's sorting himself a new playlist and lies on his back in his bunk, scrolling.

- I think it's just that they don't want us to skive off work, to hide in there. They like us out in the open where they can see us.

I hum a tune, something I only half remember and can't place. I don't know why I'm humming it. I see that Briony is already asleep. She's been quiet lately. I notice now that she's put on weight too, her hips are smooth and fleshy. I can't think why as she never stops moving, except to sleep. Maybe she's losing the skinniness of adolescence. It suits her. Dominic's gaze rests briefly on her body too.

- Do they worry we'll go into the woods for a shag? I say, Or to do drugs?

- Maybe, he snorts back. But why would we? We'd get fired straight off.

- Why don't we go look, one night?

I can't believe I'm suggesting it, it's not like me at all, but the idea just spoke itself. We'd be there with torches, crunching over leaves, the smell of the soil and that other scent, the sweetness, the arms of the shadowy trees framing the bright moon.

- No, says Dom, an odd shot of anger in his voice. He scrolls his playlist, not looking at me. Just do your job, Amber. Pollinate. You'll be out of here by autumn, travelling, like you wanted.

He's right. Why would I jeopardise my adventures for a glimpse of the woods? I turn over on my hemp pillow, close my eyes and drift into uneasy dreams.

Briony is not in the fields today. At break time I ask Dom about it. I see the citrus light of the pollen clinging to day-old stubble on his jaw. I've never noticed this before.

   - She's ill, he says, hands stuffed inelegantly into his pockets.

   - She seemed okay yesterday, I say, but as I do I remember how sleepy she's been, the slight pallor of her usually luminous skin.

   - Where do they take people when they're ill?

   - The acreage has its own doctor, I think. And somewhere quiet to go and rest. I'm sure she'll be fine.

Dom strides off to work the wildflower section, and I take the orchard to make up the numbers. If he's not worried, neither am I. The white blossoms are hanging heavy as summer cloud, longing for my contact. We work for days. We dance. We disturb the air, the pollen scattering, breezing out across the fields. The flowers long for us, rustling and inching towards our bodies. The land is shades of blue and purple, greens flickering in the distance. Everywhere: a liquid, sweet scent. Tremors become more regular. The agitated earth vibrates at least weekly, and on certain days twice. 3.2; 4.0; 4.3. A 4.6 on Thursday shakes us into nervousness for hours after, bruises us and breaks our concentration. I envy the birds and the winged midges, the metallic blue-bottles, comfortable enough in the quivering air. Dreams change. We taste each other; we are peaty-rich and sweet. The woods are always there, a cool presence at the edges of our toil. I, Amber, take one step into them one baking afternoon, accidentally, rotating against the wildflowers with my eyes closed. The ground crunches, feels instantly different, the temperature dips and our, my skin goosebumps. The pollen on my hairs flits away. I hear singing, many voices coming from the shadows. I can't make out the words. Dominic drags me back from the threshold.

   - Don't go in there. We mustn't.

And his fierce tone frightens me.

The days go on. We sleep. We dream. Scaffolding and skin. The webbing of eyelashes. Damp membranes. I crave sugar and dollop it in spoonfuls into my tea. I can pinch little handfuls of fat at my waist. I work harder than ever. Autumn is coming and we will soon be free. I'll go to Italy first to see the magnificent ruins. We will part and go about our adventures, perhaps never see one another again. And Briony is still unwell. She has not returned to us yet.

- Aren't you worried, Dom? I ask one evening before bed. He's shaving the dark shadow on his jaw. The way he does this, with such precision, makes him look older, like a man suddenly.
- She's fine. She'll be back next week.
He says it like someone who knows more than I do, and like someone who knows Briony better than I. I wonder if she has actually left, gone ahead of us. Graduated.

This morning, just as the sun was burning off the chilly mist and I was taking off my hat, there was a tremor of 5.3. The earth rumbled. Some of the crops shot down, as if pulled from underneath, back into the soil. Ungrowing. We gasped. An alarm we'd never before heard went off. It was high and urgent, and we thought for a moment that a baby or child must be amongst us, in pain, yawing for help.
- Lie flat! yelled the Overseer. Her glasses were gone, lost in the quake, and I saw her eyes clearly for the first time, big and green-black like screens. Like an insect's.
We dropped down and lay with our bellies against the earth and felt it shiver, its convulsion through the soil, like it wanted to shake us off its surface. We wondered about the city. Some of the crops on the acreage were wrecked, as if something had crushed them. We know it is only a matter of time before a 6 (damage to moderate number of well-built structures), a 7 (felt across great distances), an 8 or 9 (permanent changes in ground topography).

I feel shaken after this. We are told to return to the bunk barn and rest. My head thrums and vibrates like it's balancing on a fragile stem. My thoughts are foggy, but somehow also loud, as if I can hear static and I can't quite tune in to it. I hear snatches of music, traces of thoughts that don't seem to be mine. Perhaps they are not mine. Dom lies on his bunk staring at the ceiling. He looks flat and waxy.
- Are you scared, Dom? I admit I feel a bit scared.
He turns slowly and looks at me, his dark eyes shining.
- Don't be scared Amber. The tremors today were unusual. You're okay, aren't you?
- Yes, I say.
But I don't feel it. I don't ask about Briony today. I know the answer already. We are summoned to a special lesson shortly after this. We're told about new emergency measures to take in the event of a deeper, stronger tremor. Evasive action. The Overseer, her glasses now firmly back on the bridge of her nose, reveals some safe places for us: to the edge of the

83

acreage there is a concealed entrance, a hatch covered in wildflowers. She heaves it up and leads us down into the earth. Inside: a series of tiny pods, dark and smelling of soil and iron. Skin-smooth inside and warm to the touch.

- There are many years' worth of supplies here, she says, This is the place to come in an extreme earthquake. You will be safe here.

Safe in the dark, I think. Buried alive. If there is a tremor that bad, a tremor to rip the buildings in the city down at the root, I will stay above ground. I will not come here in the black night of the soil. I cannot. But I smile, pretend I am relieved to be so cared for, and climb the ladder back into the light. After, I return to the bunk and climb into bed, my limbs tired and hot. But I do not sleep. I can hear something in the distance and I need to follow it, to bring it into focus.

It is deep night now and I shuffle and creep, me myself, out to the acreage. I have a torch, only a weak one, but I find the moon is bright enough to see by. The calm, cool moon, is extinct and merely a mirror. Or the dusted face of a dead girl. The shadow of the woods is long and almost reaches my toes. The poppies, the dandelions, the campion are all grey-blue and don't respond to me. I hear a low hum which resolves to a murmur of voices as I approach the edge of the wood. I push through the blackberries and the rough thicket draws blood from my nakedness, but I feel no pain. Inside the wood, there is a clearing, the trees closing above. There is no source for the sounds; not the singing, clamouring group I imagined. The breeze shifts and a scent, sugared and sexual, wafts. Attached to the base of a tree is a sticky carapace, opaque and glistening in the moon's white beam. It pulses and trembles with heartbeat or breath. We see the shape of a limb flexing inside, fluid shifting, a stream of violet hair floating beneath a skin-like sack. No wonder we are not allowed to witness this. I, we, look up into the turning sky at the tiny elegies we call stars. For now, the earth is still.

LINDSAY GILLESPIE

The Last Year the Ice Lake Sang

How much does an eyelash weigh? Both his eyelids are bald now, and this is his last one.

A tonsil weighs 1.5g approx.

Last week they sliced out his tonsils (inflamed) and pulled out two molars (decayed). The doctors at the clinic believe they mess with the body's natural healing. He's asked for them back. The molars have patterns on them, like ripples; they look like tiny shells. He remembers when he used to pick up shells at Black Sand Beach and Lime Cay, on the other side of the world.

His toe nails. He peeled them off this morning before the doctors could. Something he could do himself. He has the right. This body is still his.

He has this shiny sky-blue Delta toiletry bag from the flight, where he's keeping these bits of himself. A little relic box. Eyelashes, toe nails, two molars. They haven't given him back his tonsils, not yet.

The weighing scales say eighty-eight pounds. What his twelve-year-old weighs, give or take. He will weigh eighty-two pounds, three ounces on the day he dies.

He has a rule, but today he breaks it, and looks in the mirror. Stork legs. He bunches his legs up like a lily trotter and giggles. Then the mirror shows him his locks. The more he shrinks, the more they sprout. The doctor says 'aren't they weighing you down?' He flips them up in the old man's face. They power me up, he says. Make me electric. You know I been shot, right? Nearly died right? They saved me. Stopped the bullets meant for my heart, my head. No-one gets to touch them. Only God.

Next day he finds a fallen lock crushed beneath his pillow. Lays it lengthways in the Delta bag.

The old doctor does his rounds every morning with the young doctor. They add, divide, and subtract the numbers his body is making. Every day there's a new plan for this, for that; today both doctors are shooting sweet smiles at him. How about we take a pint of blood out today. Clean it up. Then stick it back in.

'Nice try,' he says.

They tell him they're worried he's not eating.

'Must be something we can tempt you with,' they go, 'we can get our hands on most anything. Just say.'

Island food he says. Bring me dasheen, a bit of yam. And Irish moss. A cup of Irish moss.

It takes them five days to fly the Irish moss and his island food the 5,000 miles from Kingston to Munich. The trouble is snowstorms. Not in Germany. Freak snowstorms in Jamaica have paralysed the airport, shut it down. First time in thirty years.

While he's waiting, they pump infusions into his arm. Seventeen vitamins, twenty-one minerals. The doctors say it's helping, they can see an improvement. His skin feels different, looks different too. Scaly like a crayfish.

Heike is his night-shift nurse. She has white eyelashes and a blond moustache. She's all business, threading the IV tubes, cleaning, wiping, measuring, weighing. She's built big, with muscles in her cheeks, her neck.

When she's done his charts, she wheels the bed around to face the window, and drags up a chair so they're sitting side by side. She turns down the lights of the monitors, and the two of them stare out into the night. Their faces float in the window, like they're sitting on a train.

'So tell me where we're going tonight,' she asks him.

They've made little window trips all over. He always chooses the destination. Tokyo, Dakar, Addis, London, Kingston. There have been one or two football trips to watch Santos FC play, and Tottenham Hotspur. He does the commentaries, with Heike chiming in sometimes.

Their faces float in the window like two moons; his face a dark moon, hers a ghost moon.

The real moon flies about outside.

Tonight, it's the first time he hasn't named a destination. He's just sitting there. Hasn't said a word. Outside a pine-tree twitches to shake off fresh snow. He holds his hand up.

'Hear that?'

Scritch scratch.

'What's that?'

'It's a bird,' says Heike, 'An ice bird. They come with the snow, stay all Winter till the thaw.'

He asks Heike where the birds live.

'At the Ice Lake,' she says.

She goes there on her way home at the end of her shift, she says. Kurt picks her up and drives her home across the Ice Lake.

'His car's rubbish, and it's forbidden to drive on the ice,' she says, 'cars can drown.'

'He your sweetheart?'

Heike twiddles with her moustache.

'Sometimes he is,' she says, 'sometimes he's not.'

The nurse goggles her eyes.

'This town's so dead, you wouldn't believe. And winter lasts forever.'

'So Heike, you got to tell me. Is it love that you're feeling!'

She laughs.

'Kurt's an *arschgeige*. All the boys here are.'

'Arse what?'

'*Arschgeige*. It's not a good word. It means…that he is an arse violin.'

It's the first time she sees him throw his head back and laugh. She can see the sockets in his gums where his back teeth were.

'This lake. Is it far?'

'Twenty, twenty-five minutes. It's a famous lake, it's special. There's bits of it that stay frozen right to summer.'

Summer will arrive five weeks after his funeral.

'I'm sick of window trips. Take me there. I step one foot on it, it will know where I'm from. It will melt. Summer will come early.'

'Maybe,' smiles the girl, 'if you do your exercises.'

Heike heaves him up to standing. There's a big wobble, a little one, and off they lurch. They step out along the clinic's shadowy corridors, past the lab, past the old doctor's office, the consulting rooms. This part of the clinic at night is full of dead spaces. Tonight, it spooks him and he stops dead. Tells Heike he wants to turn back.

There's a surprise waiting. They've smashed his door down, his visitors. They've flown all the way to bring a bit of Jamaica to him. They've lain his Gibson Les Paul against his pillow. In nineteen days he will be buried with it propped in his left hand. The visitors tell lies, right in his face. You looking damn fine, they say, then they're all over Heike swearing they had way more snow in Kingston than here and asking how the hell you get a party started in this lockdown place in the middle of permafrost. Heike vanishes, and reappears with boxes of juices, *apfelsaft* and dumplings. The visitors are larky, tell jokes, and stupid, stupid stories. He says he's starving and holds up dumplings to his mouth before dropping them in a tangle of bedsheets and plates. He spills apple juice, guava juice, every sort of juice down his front. They plug in tapes. Listen, listen, you heard this? Check this one out, this one's new, just came out.

He calls for Heike. Get Me Out. She sweeps them out into the corridor, tells them he has to get his bloods done. Yes, even in the middle of the night. They hang in the doorway, yelling blessings at him. Heike thanks them for the visit. Says it's time for them to go. He doesn't look back.

The old doctor is away on a big trip to give talks on his newest treatment protocols, when his famous patient haemorrhages next day. From now, all visitors are verboten. He sleeps for two days and wakes in the middle of the night of the third.

Heike's waiting. Her round face shining like the moon.

She wheels his bed around so he's looking out the window.

'Look outside,'

Lights strobe the snow trees. Headlights.

Heike's friend, Anka, one of the lab nurses, is also in his room.

'We're going on a little trip,' she says.

The two nurses dress him. They thread his legs into padded trousers.

'My brother's snowsuit,' says Anke. Last thing, Heike pumps his line with a fresh dose of morphine.

They settle him in a wheelchair, bury him under a quilt.

They use the back exit. Anke has got Hermann the security guy to switch the clinic cameras off.

Outside, a crumpled blue Opel is waiting, with the engine running, making its own weather, fog and smoke. They lower him into the front seat and the driver shakes his hand and won't let go.

'This is the best night of my life,' he says.

From the back seat, more handshakes, more introductions. Someone asks for his autograph.

'We told you. No asking for stuff,' Heike's voice is all high and scratchy, 'and who the fuck asked Detlef and Uli?'

The girls start cursing out the boys.

The front seat passenger says hey, I don't mind, because he doesn't. The engine fires up and they're off, crawling along a road of old blue snow. They leave the clinic behind. He can make out church steeples and smells a farm. Goat shit. The one called Detlef says sorry, *bitte*, *danke*, excuse, and leans across him to feed a cassette into the tape deck. At minus something degrees in the shivering car, they play him 'Could You Be Loved'. On the last chorus the cassette-player eats the tape. He opens his mouth to laugh, then can't stop coughing. There's blood on his lips. Heike leans over to hold a cloth to mouth.

The Opel starts to flip-flop.

'We're on the Ice Lake,' says Kurt.

The passenger looks out. The ice lake looks like a piece of sky that's fallen down and crashed. The car wanders, then brakes.

They carry him out, settle him down on the quilts.

The nurses wrap him tight as a Christmas present. They put their fingers to their lips.

'Listen,' they say.

All around he hears the ice breathing, in, out, in and out.

The lake sighs. Then it starts to hum.

Detlef helps him crawl closer. Heike guides the side of his face to the ice. He can hear the bounce of his own blood jumping in his ears.

'Can you hear?'

He shakes his head.

Heike moves him along the blanket.

'Now?'

There's a recording studio under the ice. That's what it sounds like. He can make out the bass. A drumbeat. A shatter of cymbals.

The ice is silver cracks, like miniature lightning. These cracks ping at him from all directions. And when a crack finds him, it brings a note with it. First it sings the high notes, then it sings the low.

He wants to take a piece of the singing back with him. Lay it down in his relic box. Instead, he licks the ice.

Heike says they've stayed out way too long. They have to get back while Hermann's on duty.

Anke says so where the hell's the car. This your idea of a joke, Karl? Uli? Detlef? The girls huddle around to keep the patient warm and carry on yelling. The patient catches other words beginning with arse.

Detlef shouts. Found the car.

On the way back they keep talking to keep him awake. Karl tells him the story of the singing ice. The colder the weather, he says, the louder the singing. It was special tonight. A special performance just for him. The patient is asleep and hasn't heard a thing, but at the back door of the hospital he rouses himself to deliver a short speech.

'Arse violins. Thank you.'

The boys lift his body and carry him to his room. His temperature keeps spiking, and they can't get it down. They strip the snowsuit off him and call the emergency doctor.

Two days later he is readied for the eleven-hour flight home. He doesn't make it. He dies in a nearby country before they fly his body back home. His funeral is attended by – reports vary – 30,000 to 100,000 mourners. There are readings from the Old Testament, from the Anaphora of St John and prayers in Amharic. There are musicians, dancers and prime ministers and every kind of people. Astonishing singing. Spontaneous applause. There is tear gas.

Back at the clinic when Heike clears his room, she slips the Delta bag beneath her nurse's tunic. Hides it under her bed at home. Six months later Kurt gets with Anka and they leave Rottach Egern forever. Heike too moves on: new jobs, new boys. In one of these moves she loses the sky-blue Delta bag. From time to time when she needs the money, she forges her famous patient's signature and sells it. She recognises 'her' signatures whenever they pop up in online auctions. With the money she plans to visit his island on the other side of the world. One day.

The clinic is threatened with lawsuits and investigated. It shuts down for a year, then re-opens with the young doctor as director. The old doctor retires. The clinic's protocols still get attacked from time to time, but are no longer considered controversial. Some treatments have been discredited, whilst others have become standard practice.

The Ice Lake changes. The hard freezes are a thing of the past, and it thaws earlier and earlier. There are still calamities, and signs go up each year warning people not to risk their life.

They say 1981 was the last year the Ice Lake sang.

LARA HAWORTH

Monumenta

You're on the plane, now, and you're fine. You do up your seatbelt before they tell you to, make sure they can see it as they do their turns down the aisle. You turn off your phone, well, not exactly, that's not exactly true, is it, you put it on Airplane Mode, and it feels good to do so, the phone that has not stopped ringing for two weeks now, because you have a feeling, a very distinct, clear feeling, that two weeks following the incident, the company of which you were recently made CEO is going to throw you to the wolves, to save themselves. At first you were assured that it was not your fault, that it was legally the responsibility of Hans Kramer, your predecessor, and that was the company line, but the line has changed over the last two days, hardened and also twisted, and seems to be leading to you. You touch the rim of belly fat that sits atop the seatbelt, which feels new. The rim is new. You blame the job. You order a sparkling water. You pour it into the plastic cup and then you call down the aisle and ask for a supplementary vodka, and you pour it over the sparkling water and watch it oil its way through. You have always spoken to yourself like this, taken yourself through each day as a set of clear, discrete instructions, but before the incident it was always in the third person, *she* or *Hilde*, and now, it is moving closer, the voice, is in the second person, is *you*, both accusatory and tender, and this frightens you, or at least it did at first, but now you are just going with it, because what else can you really do. The man sitting next to you places his arm on your shared armrest and you elbow it off with one, clean movement, and he is startled and withdraws, and you are glad you still have this in you. You down the vodka and the sparkling water in two goes. Your grey suit feels tight. You close your eyes. One hour fifty minutes. Frankfurt to Belgrade. You try to sleep.

You must have slept, but have no recollection of it. No dreams. You hear the sound of the pilot, in German, then Serbian, announcing your descent. You think of your mother, and you feel something move in your stomach, and you wonder if you are hungry. You want a croissant. The sky outside the aeroplane window is blue. The towers of Belgrade look solid. The rivers look thirsty. You are thirsty. You want a coffee. Something stronger. You think of your brother. You will be kind to him. You will try. The new voice has the air of Biblical Commandments. This amuses you, because when you were a child, you were convinced that angels had wires that went into your head and read your thoughts and beamed them up to heaven and you used to lie in bed and think, *she hates God, she hates God*, and then try to undo it, *she's sorry, she's sorry*, but the hating voice would always come back, stronger, more resilient, than the one that asked for forgiveness. You confessed this to your father one day, as you waited to go to school. He was volcanically angry and accused your mother of sending you to church in secret, which she hadn't, you got the idea of angels and God from your grandmother, who had you christened in secret, and you hadn't told anyone, ever, and you still hated God, on balance.

You disembark the plane. You say to yourself, *You are home*, but it does nothing. You are an exile. You have no home. You sound melodramatic. You touch the sides of the walls as you walk to passport control. You practise saying the words printed on them in Serbian, under your breath. *Toilets. Visit Historic Belgrade. Emergency Exit*. Your breath feels bad in your mouth. You hold out your two passports to the man at the booth: German, Serbian. You let him decide what you are. He selects the Serbian one, and says, *Welcome home*, but doesn't sound as though he means it. He sounds angry, in fact. Or perhaps bored. You skip baggage reclaim because you have no baggage, which is, in one sense, a profound lie, and this pleases you. You buy a croissant and eat it as you withdraw cash from the ATM, EUROLINK, flakes of pastry settling on the keypad and the front of your suit. You can't remember the exchange rate. All of the suggested amounts seem ludicrously large. You receive what seems to be three thousand worn notes from the slot. You roll them into a thick slice and put them in your suit pocket. You feel your phone in the other pocket. You leave it on Airplane Mode. You exit the airport automatic doors into a steam bath of cigarette smoke, you decide not to speak their language. You summon a taxi driver in English and he asks if you have any baggage and you say no, and again feel privately pleased, as if you have got away with a grand deceit.

You give your mother's address in English, and the taxi driver makes for the motorway into the city and won't stop talking in broken English about how Serbian women are the most beautiful women in the world, how Serbian caviar is the most beautiful in the world, asks you if you know this, if you have ever been here before. You ignore him. Your suit has damp patches under the arms. The croissant flakes have left pallid stains on the breast. The motorway singles out into a road, the taxi driver leans out of the window and shouts something homophobic at another driver that he thinks you don't understand, you start to recognise the landscape. The lilacs are out. People are walking their dogs, drinking coffee outside cafés, the city feels smarter than you remember. You pass shops, stop at a red light. A window full of tracksuits catches your eye. One in particular. Diadora. Electric blue, with pink and purple shapes up the arms, at the ends of the legs. Made of something shiny. You ask the taxi driver, in English, to pull over. He doesn't understand, or ignores you. He moves on from the traffic light, now green, away from the tracksuit. You repeat yourself, in English, then German, then Mandarin. He won't listen. You command him, in a stream of unbroken Serbian that falls out of your mouth as the truest, easiest thing you've ever said, to turn around, right now, and take you back to the tracksuit. He turns for a moment, shocked, to take you in, does an illegal manoeuvre in the middle of the street and returns you to the shop.

You go into the shop and purchase the Diadora tracksuit immediately, peeling off notes from the roll in your pocket. It costs several thousand of them. You have no idea what they amount to. You take the tracksuit into the changing room and put it on, look at yourself in the mirror. Your yellow hair is thinning and dry, your face, angled and pointed for business, has lost weight, your rim of belly fat is concealed by the tracksuit, your eyes have lost their studied blankness, seem sharper, as if they're seeing something very specific. You look different. You remove the remaining banknotes from your grey trouser suit, zip them up into your new, shiny electric-blue pockets, and take the grey suit to the counter. You know it still has your phone in its pocket. You ask them to throw it away. In Serbian.

You emerge from the shop and get back into the taxi. The taxi driver is laughing hysterically and banging his fist on the steering wheel. *Oh, now I've seen it all!* He is weeping. *Now I have! Welcome home! Look at you! You look fantastic! You will slip seamlessly into this unbroken stream of Slavs!* He drives you with a new fervour towards Dedinje, the old neighbourhood, to your mother's house. To your old house. To the house where you grew up. He seems so excited, you feel he might wind down the window and announce your return to everyone passing by, set off some fireworks from the driver's side, sound an alarm.

Your taxi driver does, in fact, herald your arrival, sounding his car horn in one, long, unbroken wail as you pull up outside the house. It wakes your brother and mother, underneath the cherry tree, although you will only find this out later, when your brother takes you aside to tell you how worried he is. He will tell you he found your mother there, sleeping, earlier in the morning, and that he had also found her under the table on the terrace when he arrived, four days previously. He will press his hand against his eye and tell you he is afraid she is losing her mind, that that morning he had decided to lie down next to her, under the cherry tree, to try and normalise this alarming, irregular sleep pattern. You will, as always, find his quiet solicitousness towards your mother irritating and painful all at once.

He will tell you that she said, *This is nice*, as she woke, looking across at him, that she had the crushed remains of some purple flowers by her side, and that she attributed the car horn of your taxi driver to her *demented neighbour*.

He will tell you that he winced at the word, *demented,* that she went on to describe how every time this neighbour has a fight with his wife he goes out to the car and leans on the horn until everyone in the street is angry, as well.

'Collective responsibility,' your brother said, getting up and pulling your mother to her feet, walking together around the side of the house, to the terrace, to watch you exit your taxi and walk in the front gate, which is when your realities merge, for the first time in seven years.

'Nice tracksuit!' shouts your brother.

The house looks down at you with its 1930s limestone slab face, impassive. You try to remember the last time you looked up at it. The only memories that come, your back is to it, walking away.

'No luggage?' says your mother, walking down the concrete steps to greet you. You notice the imperfection of her chignon, a stray leaf caught in her hairline, which you will not fully understand until later.

'No baggage,' you say, and to your mother's surprise, you can feel it, a small spasm in her muscles, you bow your frame around your mother's shoulders and hold on, very tightly. You can smell your new tracksuit as you bring its arms around her: fresh manufacturing, the inside of a new car.

'Welcome home,' says your mother, patting your head. You are still clinging on. 'I dreamt about you last night. I had no idea you were such a good dancer.'

You pull back from the embrace and look at your mother, remembering your face in the tracksuit shop mirror. 'I'm not. I'm hungry.'

You have breakfast on the terrace. Your brother and mother sense that you, *Hilde*, shockingly, need looking after, need tending to, and they disappear to prepare the food and make the coffee with a seriousness that feels like a novelty to everyone, because you are sitting very still on the terrace with very pale hands laid flat on the red Formica table, staring out across the street, at nothing, in an electric-blue tracksuit.

Your mother makes you up a plate from the things they bring to the table, a boiled egg, some salami, tomatoes, börek with yoghurt, some cherries. She tells you about the architect Karl Hobeek's proposal to demolish the house and leave a crater, which reminds you why you're here. Your mother's house, the one where you grew up, has been requisitioned by the city to be turned into a monument. *To the massacre.* You almost ask if anyone has yet decided which massacre they will memorialise, but stop yourself. It leads you too swiftly to your own. Too late. You spill some seeds from the tomatoes you have been eating down your front. You feel your mother watching you eat, then fail to eat correctly. You can understand why: historically, you have not really eaten. Refused to as a baby, and then, as you got older, only in tiny amounts, as though there was a finite supply you were preserving for something, some future catastrophe. Which may well be now. Your plate is suddenly empty. You grasp the spoon in the bowl of yoghurt and pick it up, but your hand shudders in mid-air and it falls to the ground. You see your brother glance at your mother, who bends down to pick up the spoon. Your brother fills up your plate again and moves back quickly into his chair, as if he's filled the bowl of a hungry wild animal, unsure of how it will react. You keep on eating, nodding in places as your mother elaborates on Karl Hobeek, on the preposterous nature of memorialising the death of King Alexander Obrenovic, the one with stupid glasses.

'You didn't tell me that, about his glasses,' says your brother. 'Do you think they were smashed in the fall?'

Apparently King Alexander Obrenovic was assassinated and thrown over his own balcony.

'I don't know, probably,' says your mother.

You keep eating as your brother takes over the story of Misha Popovic, the second architect who has visited your mother's house to pitch for a monument. *Misha*, your brother says, breathlessly, wants to install a shopping mall, *the ugliest building in the world*, that will encase their home, both erased and preserved for some indeterminate future. Do you understand what he intends to memorialise, he asks you. He's not testing you, he's too kind for that, he's ascertaining the clarity of Misha's idea. You shake your head. *Yugoslavia*, he says. He seems high, or dumbstruck, as he says this.

'Misha seems to have made quite an impression on you,' says your mother.

Your plate is empty again and before you can do anything the proposed realities of Karl Hobeek's crater and Misha Popovic's ugliest building in the world converge to crush upon you your actual reality, which is to say, the incident, the thing that has happened and is still happening, which is you, and the company of which you are – were – still might be – CEO, in the course of building three high-rise, mixed-use towers on the site of an old park on the outskirts of Frankfurt, witnessing, precipitating, through negligence or fate or timetabling or the wrong kind of earth, the collapse of its very deep foundations, and the burial of ten workers, only seven of who were found alive.

You realise that you are crying. You aren't moving or emitting any sound, but tears, nonetheless, are coming down your face. Your mother looks astonished, you can see her trying to remember the last time she saw you cry. She takes off her sunglasses and puts them on you, as if she is not sure who is more afraid to look. You can feel tears that won't stop appearing from beneath the dark frames.

'Hilde, what's wrong?' says your brother, his voice tender. You see him turn to your mother and mouth the question, *Yugoslavia?*, which would have made you laugh, if everything were different.

'Now, tell me, Hilde,' says your mother. 'Do you remember when you would sit in the hallway and wait to go to school? Six in the morning, in your smart clothes, with your books in your bag. Even on holidays. Just, waiting, until you could go?'

You remain very still, tears still coming. They itch. You had forgotten this.

'You were a big shot even then. And you're a big shot now.'

'I'm just very sad,' you say.

'Well, show me,' your mother says, moving closer, and lifting the sunglasses up at an angle, so they rest on your forehead. 'Show me what a sad big shot looks like.'

Your mother chops lamb liver and beef shin into mince, criss-crosses it, finely, at angles, cuts down an onion, some garlic, adds salt, fries it.

You, Hilde, sit at the kitchen table, still in your Diadora tracksuit, drinking red wine, watching her.

'This is my favourite knife,' says your mother, holding it above her head as she adds paprika to the pan, some tomato puree. Your mother talks with confidence, inhabiting the unusual space you are permitting her for story, for anecdote. She seems puffed, plumped somehow, by you needing her. Do you need her? Does she, Hilde need her? Is this what this is?

'Oh,' you say.

It is evening, your mother is preparing dinner in your childhood kitchen, which has aged, badly, in the seven years since you were last here. The cabinets are flaking blue paint, the orange lino bulging and torn, the lace half-curtains stained. It seems to be on the verge of collapse. You have stopped crying, had a shower, put the tracksuit back on, had a nap.

Your brother has taken you aside and told you he is worried your mother is losing her mind. You have been watching for signs, but have not seen any.

'Since a child, this knife.' Your mother shows you the handle, which is a dark, mottled wood, worn down in places, as if with water.

'Since a child, you had a knife.'

Your mother nods, adding rice and water to the mince and onions. 'Now, the peppers,' she says, moving towards the fridge, lifting one leg high and stepping over something midway. Something that is not there.

'What was that?' you say.

Your brother, sitting cross-legged on one of the counters, by the sink, turns from where he is leaning out of the window, smoking. He looks at you with a look, and the look says, *See*?

'What was what?' your mother says.

'That, then. What did you just step over?'

'Oh.' Your mother looks down. 'Your father.'

Your father died in this kitchen. Seven years ago. His heart was too big. Not in an emotional way, but in a medical way.

You feel your brother urging you to say something, something you might have said, if everything were different. *Stop that at once*, or, *We're going to the hospital*. But instead a wave of pressure bulges behind your eyes. Are you going to cry again? Where has Hilde gone?

'It's OK, I'm used to it,' says your mother, pulling out peppers from the fridge, stepping over the ghost of your father's body on the floor as she returns to the stove.

'And what about this sleeping, Mama,' says your brother, giving up on you, and on his hope that you will provide some difficult order. He tries to take your place but his voice falters. 'The table on the terrace, the cherry tree...'

Your mother waves a hand in the air, so dismissively, with such authority, it vapourises the question of her losing her mind. 'I've been having the most fantastic dreams.'

'Night terrors?' says your brother, his golden face paling.

Your brother has, his whole life, suffered from night terrors. You used to think he was pathetic, weak. Now you wonder if he was just earlier to discover some essential truth of the world, while you were – what were you doing? Business.

'No,' says your mother, her voice pleasant. 'Dreams.' She begins scoring each pepper, green, off at the top, pulling the seeds out with the tip of her knife, rooting out the bitter black stalks that lurk underneath. 'I used to take my knife to state dinners. Your father thought I was mad. I

97

put it in my handbag, underneath my tissues. It made me feel strong.' She touches the blade. 'Ukrainian steel.'

Your brother brings over the pan of mince and rice from the stove to the table and you sit with the uncapped peppers, stuffing each one until it is full.

You lift a hand to your hair to push it out of the way and leave a trail of mincemeat across your forehead. 'I buried several men,' you say, to the table. 'I buried several men alive.'

'Where?' says your brother, very intensely, his eyes wide.

'In Frankfurt,' you say.

'Not to worry, Hilde,' says your mother, with a tone of calm efficiency.

You can sense what your mother is thinking, or perhaps you can't, perhaps it is you, thinking this, in your old, third person voice. *Whatever it is, Hilde will deal with it.*

You look over at your brother, frozen, mid-pepper, one fist full of mince, his face an old, bed-soaked night terror, padded and wounded, knowing that if he had said this, your mother would have been already getting up from the table and onto a flight to Frankfurt, to clear up his mess, to make it right. But it is you, Hilde, who has been trained to fix her own problems, even if they are, by your own admission, quite large.

'I'm sure you will find a way to fix this,' your mother says.

'Hilde, are you going to be arrested,' says your brother, in a quiet voice.

'Serbia's extradition treaty with the EU is under considerable strain at the moment,' says your mother, stuffing a pepper in one movement.

'We were building a set of high-rise, mixed-use towers on an old park. The crater collapsed. The foundations collapsed. I saw it. Mama.' *Mama.* Something is happening to your language, to your Serbian, it is regressing, becoming childlike, the accusing, tender, relentless, *you, you, yous,* pulled in confusing directions between *I* and *she* and *Hilde* and *you.* Perhaps this is what being at home means. An exhausting fight over perspective.

Your mother, surprised by your use of the word, *Mama,* wears a look that tells you to pull yourself together and submit to her help, all at once. 'You could always stay here.'

The doorbell rings.

You and your brother put your hands over your mouths in unison and gasp, or laugh, or cry. It is unclear. Your brother looks like a tiny ghost. Is this what you look like?

'Pull yourselves together,' says your mother, and leaves the kitchen, wiping her hands on her apron, which, once she has her back to you and is walking away, you see covers a gold lamé dress.

'Hilde, do you know this woman,' your mother says, returning to the kitchen, followed by the visitor.

It is the woman from the tracksuit shop. You hadn't remembered how young she is, her face a fresh dumpling, ears piled high with gold earrings, her hair oily and dark and moussed to the top of her head.

'Wow it smells like my grandmother's,' the woman from the tracksuit shop says, looking around the kitchen, confusedly, as if she's fallen backwards into the past. She remembers herself, pulls out your grey trouser suit from the plastic bag around her wrist, and from its pocket, your phone. 'Sorry to call so late, but you left this.' She lays it down on the table, beside the peppers. 'That tracksuit really looks great on you.'

With your new perspective, you can tell she is lying.

'How did you find us?' says your brother, his hand on his chest.

'In the other pocket.' She pulls out a piece of paper, places it next to the phone. In your handwriting, under the heading 'Home / Not Home', the address of the house.

'A real detective,' says your mother, and laughs, and the laugh sounds like a lid placed over a pan that is on fire. She pours the woman a glass of wine, gestures to the peppers. 'We're preparing a dinner. A big one.'

'These also remind me of my grandmother,' says the woman, picking up an empty pepper and beginning to stuff it, contentedly.

You stare at her, amazed at how some people are at home wherever they are.

'Now, Hilde, is this your phone from – ' says your mother.

You nod, you give in. You know what your mother will do later, what you will all do. You will take the phone out into the garden, dig a hole with the long-handled spade, and bury it. But what you don't know, or aren't expecting, is the way your mother will first take the spade and turn it so the tip of the handle faces towards the ground, before bringing it down, hard, on the face of the phone, destroying it in three blows.

MALCOLM HEYHOE

Hatches Before They Chicken

They were melting in the living room of Lena's house, a candle flickering for St Dympna, the protector of Polish widows' bank accounts.

Listen to this, said Katy, reading from a magazine.

In marriage, what has been your deepest pleasure?

Her boyfriend Harry was about to pick his nose

Having my knickers taken down by my husband, said Katy.

What kind of gibbertyflibbert says such crazy things? said Lena. A floosy woman!

Katerina Theresa Wackowski was Katy, and her mother was Lena the terrible. Never tiring of telling everyone how foreign she'd felt from the day she landed in England, a displaced person from Poland, and her adopted country a strange place where the people kept fridges switched on in winter and young women wore knickers, yes, knickers, with a string at the back and Katy spending her adult life putting a hand over her mouth whenever Lena let fly one of her famous zingers.

Zinger number one:

Katerina, please tell me, what is the point of ducks?

After the knickers down business, Katy and Harry had tempted Lena from her little fortress for an afternoon stroll and returning from a desultory amble around a country park, Lena had let rip on the ducks.

I think they're rather cute, said Katy.

That hair on top of head, give me scissors to cut it, said Lena.

Please, not that stiff little spike, said Harry. So charming.

Lena looked to the sky and said in a wistful tone, can you not see things as they are?

Later, they stopped at a popular pizza place for a tasty bite to eat. They should have known better. Happily, duck was not to be found anywhere on the menu.

Katy, said Lena, what is this?

Lena held aloft a slice of deep-crust pizza topped with extra peppers.

Mother, please, there are people eating around us.

Zinger number two:

Is just a bit of bread? said Lena.

100

Eat your pizza, mother, said Katy. People are staring.

And they kept on staring, hunkered down behind their menus.

I make you this at home, Lena said, then we don't have to pay for someone else's bits of bread.

She dropped the offending pizza slice onto her plate with a plop. Harry, kind Harry, was paying for the meal, and this was not what he wanted to hear.

Zinger number three:

Crazy to charge so much money for bit of bread.

Mum, please, at least have some salad and look there's salad dressing too, said Katy.

Lena picked up the dressing.

Looks like urine, said Lena, her cheeks glowing. Old man's urine.

Back home and mother, daughter, and prospective son-in-law hugged each other on the doorstep of Lena's modest home, and Lena once again gave the young people strict instructions for their compulsory attendance at Lena's seventy-eighth birthday party at the Polish Community Centre on Saturday.

And you, Johnny bloody Lennon Elvis Presley, said Lena, jabbing a finger at Harry's chest. Bring your guitar. There will be Polish dancing music. I would like you to play at my birthday.

But mother, Harry plays rock music, said Katy, dumbfounded.

It is all the same, said Lena. Music, music, music. Let him play.

They remained on the doorstep, three stooges in the fading light.

See, the shadows are longer and the dews heavy, said Lena. Like in Polska.

Lena threw back her head, her face flush with memories. Harry thought she looked less crazy but resembled instead a preacher summoning up spirits from the dead. Lena's house backed onto the park, and they heard the dying shrieks of children playing on the swings.

What is the name of the band playing at your birthday bash? said Harry.

Bash, said Lena, what is this bash you are talking about?

It's a turn of phrase, said Katy.

Party, Harold, it is a birthday party not a bash and if anyone is hitting people over the head then that will be me. Bash, bash, bash.

Mother don't call my future husband Harold. He's Harry, said Katy.

Mrs Wackowski, said Harry, what is the name of the band playing in your honour on Saturday?

Lenny Boniek and the Polska Boys, said Lena, proudly. Hot stuff.

Can't say I've heard of them, said Harry.

World famous, Harold, in Polish circles, said Lena. Accordion player is genius.

That's nice, mum, said Katy. Getting a band to play for people on your birthday.

They don't deserve it, said Lena. All grabbing bastardy. Every one of them.

Lena winked at Harry to let him know this was one of her little jokes.

Accordion player is Lenny from Wroclaw. Polish prodigy, said Lena.

Seven-thirty then, said Katy, on the dot. We shall see you there.

Zinger number four:

If I make it that is, said Lena.

Hang on, said Katy, but it's your seventy-eighth birthday bash, sorry, party. You can't sit at home and leave everyone in the lurch.

Lurch, said Lena. What is this lurch? Is it like, a church?

Mother, don't you dare not turn up or I will kill you with my bare hands.

Katy growled and put both hands around her mother's throat.

Go ahead, said Lena. Kill me. Then I can join Alfonse.

Alfonse's picture sat at an angle in the front window of Lena's semi, the edges curling pointedly so the wedding-suited young Pole of fifty years ago disappeared incrementally before everyone's eyes. In the late afternoon, Lena would move to the little armchair by the window to sit beside Alfonse's black and white portrait.

God willing, I shall be there, said Lena, raising her bobble-hatted head to the heavens, God looking down on the widow Lena Wackowski through the clouds and giving her his blessing and wasn't that Alfonse playing cards and drinking slivovitz in the background with the frisky angels? If so, then Alfonse should get back down to earth, thought Lena, where I want him to be, but she knew there was no coming back for the boy from the Zakopane mountains. Death was a one-way ticket.

In England, Lena lived in a world of kohlrabi sliced and buttered, miniature glasses of Bison vodka and the heady aroma of strong-smelling stews that cooked for days and lasted for weeks, and monumental Polish cheesecakes that contributed to significant weight gains only partly offset by country rambles dedicated to the surreptitious harvesting of blackberries in summer.

When you meet my mum, be prepared for anything, Katy warned Harry when she first took him home. Alfonse was alive back then but sadly he exerted no influence upon his wife's eccentric behaviour. If anything, his doleful presence merely egged his wife on to bolder and more outrageous outbursts.

No, I shall be there on Saturday if I am alive, said Lena.

But surely Mrs W, said Harry. You're not planning on leaving us anytime soon.

I am Lena, please, said Lena. What is with this Mrs Double-U? And no, I don't plan on dying in the next few days, but God moves in mysterious ways, and I am not counting my hatches before they chicken.

Harry was laughing. Chickens before they hatch, Mrs W.

Lena ignored his correction. Before you go, did I tell you Anthony Lebowski has only days to live. Poor man.

Lena made the sign of the cross upon her chest and Katy exchanged strained looks with Harry.

If God takes Anthony Lebowski by Thursday, said Lena, then he can make work with his own idle hands, and I might be next. If I die before Saturday, Katy, please inform your sister in that shitey puke hole of America. My son Ziggy knows what kind of coffin I want. And don't forget to water my beans and tomatoes. I do not want them rotting away when I'm gone and remember the key for the coal hole is behind the cuckoo clock and my bank book is in the third drawer down, in the big chest opposite the television. Be warned, there are spare under blooms inside. Don't look. And I don't want Father Michael Aloysius to take my funeral service. The man has beard and smells of that stinky cologne, and he needs to put on another stone. And another thing...

Harry and Katy waved goodbye to Lena before making their escape down the garden path.

Do you think the German Army was to blame for my mum and how she is? said Katy, sitting up in bed later that evening.

Who knows, said Harry, but her life can't have been easy.

Mum was a peasant really from peasant stock, and she would never have left Poland if the Nazis hadn't invaded and taken over her village.

Harry tried to imagine Lena's alternative life if she had stayed behind in Poland and there had not been a Second World War. He got as far as seeing geese scurrying around a settlement of thatched dwellings, smoke burning from an open fire and pigs honking from a nearby pen. In the middle of this semi-rural mayhem, he heard Lena Wackowski complaining to a gap-toothed old man about a birthday bash. Bash, bash, bash she was shouting at the top of her voice in competition with the squealing pigs.

England wasn't even Lena's first choice of new country when the war was over, and she was designated a displaced person. Katy remembered Lena remarking that Canada was her first choice of a fresh home. All those prairies, Lena said. Those big hunt balls in country houses and the farms and the giant skies. Instead, she landed in England, shipped off to the East Midlands, the humble provincial city of Nottingham.

She does like you, said Katy, fluffing up her pillow.

And I love her dearly, said Harry.

Don't be sarcastic.

If she loves me, she has a funny way of showing it.

All her ways are funny.

Really, she's a monster.

I know, it's awful but what can we do.

Wait for her to die.

And I am the youngest daughter of a monster.

Which makes me the monster's son-in-law.

I'm not like her, am I? said Katy, helplessly.

Harry shook his head.

Can you see why my sister left for America as soon as she had the money for the plane fare.

Basia Wackowski lived in New York, on the Lower East Side. She had graduated with a first-class degree in Fashion from Central St Martin's and flown to America after landing a dream job with Gap just three days after her graduation ceremony. Lena refused to attend on the grounds that London was a den of iniquity and the train prices from Nottingham to the capital amounted to daylight robbery of two Polish persons of modest means. Alfonse, who worked on the butchery counter of a local supermarket, had dearly wanted to witness his eldest daughter's graduation, but was placed under house arrest by Lena for the duration of the ceremony and after-party. Alfonse's sudden death from a heart attack – God working long hours on that fateful Wednesday – had left Katy in pieces for a long time after and she carried around in her mind the best memories of her father, quiet and uncomplaining and hurrying to the door with a broad smile on his face whenever Katy came to call, asking for Harry too but happy to draw his youngest daughter close, a precious ally and a refuge in his lifelong war with Lena.

Who the hell are Lenny Boniek and the Polska Boys? said Harry.

God knows, said Katy. But one thing's for sure all the boys will be about ninety years old, sporting moustaches, wearing waistcoats, and taking vodka shots before, during and after each song.

So, it will be a short set.

A miniature.

What if the singer gets so drunk, said Harry, and he takes a running jump and demolishes the drumkit like Kurt Cobain did with that kamikaze leap when Nirvana played the Reading Festival.

And busts his shoulder. A dumb thing to do, said Katy. And what if the drummer is like Keith Moon?

It was Harry's turn to laugh. Hell no, I can see him now, some sweaty doughball hammering ten tons of grief out of that drumkit and Lenny belting out an outrageous wedding song. But what if Lenny drums and sings at the same time?

Katy extended her toes.

And you, my darling, will climb onstage for a cameo performance to commemorate the seventy-eighth birthday bash, bash, bash of Lena Wackowski. In the year, 2005.

Lena the monster.

Shall I put out the light? said Katy.

One more thing, said Harry. I read the other day about the vast amount of vodka shots people drink during a Polish wedding. I believe it is one of the great unanswered questions of the day.

Thousands, said Katy, snuggling down among the sheets.

Apparently, it is impossible to come up with an accurate count as the glasses are refilled immediately and the shots are sunk one after the other.

Drunken Polish bastardy, said Katy, and Harry slipped down beside her, smiling.

Do you think I should get fitted for a waistcoat ahead of my guest spot with Lenny What-sis-name and the Polska Dots?

Katy wasn't listening but snoring instead.

Lena Wackowski's birthday bash went with a steady swing. Guests slipped through a tiny vestibule into a medium-sized hall hung with welcoming streamers and coloured balloons. Perhaps fifty people clustered around tables in tightly packed groups. Upon a small stage squatted a rudimentary drumkit, the name Lenny and the Polska Dots stencilled across the bass drum. The more sharp-eyed observers spotted a sheet-music stand for the accordion-player.

Rosol, a popular Polish broth (soup of the devil according to Lena) was served as a first dish followed by a buffet of hams, cheeses, meats, stinking salami slices, vegetable jellies, salads, and other kinds of cold and warm snacks. Most of the guests matched Lena in age (if not temperament) but several small boys and girls, most with chubby thighs and day-old haircuts ducked and dived between the tables, the legs of adults like trees in a thickly forested jungle, handbags on the floor becoming crocodiles for tiny feet to dodge around in the hall.

Are they eating again? asked Lena, withering those guests at the buffet table with a frown. She was wearing a smart green dress, her best frock, and everyone who greeted Lena agreed she looked well for her age. On top of whole world, Jadwiga Penkovy toasted, and Lena sadly a widow, as everyone knew, but one who had remained faithful in her heart to long departed Alfonse and that was a blessing.

Old friends piled their plates mountain high and winked like sly conspirators. Lena's tightness with money was legendary and made her the saint of stinginess in the eyes of some Polish folk. Tonight's largesse had left many friends open-mouthed and wondering if Lena was right in her mind. How many marbles has she lost?

Harry and Katy sat by Lena's side, faithful lieutenants to the monster, thought Harry, or minders, consigliere perhaps with a whiff of the Mafioso about Lena's more whiplash pronouncements.

Look, said Lena, have they not eaten for days, starving themselves for this moment when they can stuff their mushes with food paid for and provided by me, Lena Wackowski, the birthday girl. See, Kamel Glick, he is so thin he has been on hunger strike for the big day. Bastard!

Mum, who is that nice man waving at us from over there? said Katy. She wanted to wave back.

Don't look, said Lena, we don't want to encourage him over here.

He's still waving, said Katy. I think he's coming over.

Bastardy, bastardy, bastardy! said Lena.

Hi there, said Harry, we meet again.

He held out his hand for the man to shake.

Remember the name, said the man, Lenny Boniek. One of the best. Beatles rubbish.

Hello, said Katy.

Sylvester, you pimple, said Lena. Smoking again.

Sylvester Lato was bald with a hole the six of a sixpence on the top of his head. He lived alone in a decrepit bungalow and had known Lena from the time she had married Alfonse, carrying a torch for Lena back in those barely forgotten carefree days.

We met out the back, said Harry. I was just grabbing some air and Sylvester was enjoying a cigarette.

Sylvester rolled his own furnace-like ciggies.

No one enjoys smoking, said Lena. Sylvester, I can smell it on you.

Lena, my dear, said Sylvester. You look lovely tonight. Happy birthday!

To everyone's surprise he leaned in for a courageous kiss, but Lena dipped left and ended up wrapping arms around Sylvester in a primitive bear hug that promptly became a citizen's arrest leaving her long-term ardent suitor exposing a ripple of belly as he was hauled across the table by Lena's strong arms.

You have thin lips, said Lena, like a dachshund!

A happy time for all, said Sylvester, Lena letting go. So many nice people and so much nice food. Lena, there is goodness in your heart.

I hope you haven't eaten too much, said Lena.

Sylvester patted his considerable belly.

Only what I need.

So, plenty of plates then, said Lena. You will get fatter.

Mother don't say that about Sylvester. It's rude.

Katerina, that's her way, said Sylvester. She has the tongue of a viper, but I know she has a good heart.

Rubbish, said Lena. Do I hear violins?

A string quartet, perhaps, said Harry.

He is a fine young man, said Sylvester, turning to Katy. Take good care of him.

Oh, I will, I will, said Katy.

Johnny bloody Lennon, said Lena. Do you know he is playing for us tonight?

You must marry this man, said Sylvester.

Stop, said Lena, do not give the young people ideas.

Sylvester chuckled.

Who knows, Lena, my lovely, but maybe you too will marry again and walk down the aisle.

Wow, said Harry. I feel a proposal coming on. Hey, why don't we have a double wedding ceremony?

Rubbish, said Lena. Rubbish, rubbish, rubbish! I will be dead and a widower for eternity and that will be that.

Lena, my lovely, don't say that to me, said Sylvester. I shall eat more ham and then there will be more of me for you to get hold of, because your arms are so strong.

He has tattoo, said Lena, looking disappointed. What did I read, how the tattoo is an emblem of hollow spirit – somebody wrote this in newspaper.

It happened when I was young and serving in Polish army, said Sylvester.

And beards too, said Lena. They have enormous potential for destruction.

But your son, Ziggy, has a perfectly nice goatee beard, said Katy.

His soul is rotten and no good will come of that beard, said Lena. If I should catch him sleeping, I would shave off every, last hair from his chin.

Mother, said Katy, sometimes I think you are crazy.

There was a commotion on the tiny stage as Lenny and his two Polska Dots made their entrance.

Does he need a Zimmer frame? asked Harry.

The band looked about two hundred years old. Lenny's accordion hung on his chest like a heart machine. The drummer and double-bass player took their positions in slow time, the double-bassist helped to the stage on the arm of the drummer, fussing with his nostril hair.

I think they've come back from the dead, said Harry.

I heard that, said Lena.

It's a joke, mum, said Katy.

Very funny, said Sylvester, whistling through his tobacco teeth.

Hello and good evening, said the singer, barely audible between several small coughs. We are Lenny and the Polska Dots.

Lenny had false teeth and Polska Dots sounded from Lenny's mouth like poky spots.

Then he said, more loudly, happy birthday, Lena Wackowski!

The drummer smashed a cymbal.

One hundred years, one hundred years, Lenny let rip, unaccompanied. May you live one hundred years.

He waved his arms in the air and dropping to one knee, he rose with a rose between his teeth, and everyone in the hall joined in with great verve and gusto butchering the traditional Polish celebration song, 'Sto Lat', sung on birthdays and weddings and wishing the newly wedded couple a happy one hundred years.

Once again, once again, may you live a hundred years, sang Lenny.

Lena, said Sylvester, standing before Lena and proposing a toast. May you live to a hundred and prosper!

He raised his vodka glass. People cheered. Children clapped.

May I die before I should have to live until a hundred, said Lena.

God, mother, said Katy, there is no hope for you.

Katy do not take God's name in vain, said Lena. He is listening. He will punish you.

There is no God, said Sylvester, and his courtship of Lena went up in flames.

Godmother sounded just about right for Lena, thought Harry and he slung down two stiff vodka shots in readiness for his cameo role with Lenny and the lads. The band played mostly Polish songs including a tribute to the great Polish astronomer, Copernicus, and Lenny's increasingly fancy accordion frills persuaded the younger audience members (those still in their sixties and seventies) to shuffle onto the dance floor.

Look at them, said Lena. In Poland they would be queueing for milk and hitting each other with shopping bag.

If this was a wedding, said Sylvester, the groom would lift the bride over his head, catch her by the waist and spin her around the dance floor.

Katy looked at Harry.

Don't worry, darling, if we get married, I don't expect you to sweep me off my feet and spin me around the dance floor.

Sylvester sank another shot of vodka.

Lena, my lovely, if we were to marry, I would lift you off the floor and spin you in the air, my gorgeous bride. Shall we dance?

And I would be dead, you silly old fool, said Lena, under blooms showing before my feet touched the ground.

But being dead, said Harry, isn't that what you want from life?

An old man wielding a cane approached Lena's table, a sturdy tortoise in motion, as if he might sink to the floor and take a nap after every step taken.

May the ground open and swallow me, said Lena on seeing the old man and his cane.

He wore a long black leather coat and peaked cap and as he lifted his stick to greet Lena, Harry was uncomfortably reminded of the Waffen SS.

Lena, greetings on your birthday and may you live long, and may the Russkis perish as I stand here before you.

Boguslav, I thought you weren't well, said Lena. Go home, you look terrible.

See, said Boguslav, looking to Harry and Kate for mutual support, how funny she is, not like Russki, who are evil. Pure evil.

He is from mountain folk. He sleeps with an axe under his pillow, said Lena.

Boguslav was eighty-three. He lived alone (and yes, with an axe beneath his pillow) and he ate his meals straight from the saucepan.

I am having nightmares still, he said. Russkis come and burn down our village and take me away. Russki is bastardy!

He waved his cane violently, carving a dangerous arc, Harry, and Sylvester ducking in fear of decapitation while Katy and Lena remained safe on the other side of the table.

Sit down, you old fool, said Lena, and enjoy the music.

Katy poured him a drink.

Putin, I spit on his name. New leader, he was K.G.B, said Boguslav, scowling as he sat.

Putin is pillock, said Lena. Showing always his chest.

And why, said Boguslav, only sixty-six Poles on the Windrush?

There was more kerfuffle from the stage.

Now we have a guest to introduce, said Lenny. A very special guest – so let's hear a big round of applause for Mr Harry Keen, a rock and roll star and the future law-in-son of Lena Wackowski, the beautiful birthday girl.

The drummer sang happy birthday again and smashed the cymbals.

How I miss Alfonse, said Lena. He was terrific dancer and taught his cousins how to knot a bow tie.

Our blood is Polish forever, said Sylvester, and he seized Lena's hand and squeezed it.

Harry made his way through the crowd and climbed to the stage. The drummer smashed the cymbals and shouted in Polish. Some of the crowd roared and laughed. Lenny smiled and made rapid, spell-binding movements with his fingers and the music flowed more freely.

Thank you, Lenny, said Harry, standing sheepishly.

He'd left his guitar case by the double-bassist's spot and eagerly retrieving his favourite instrument he held his beloved Honda acoustic in his hands.

Do you know Rolling Stones? asked Lenny, heat rushing to his face and his veiny eyes peering mistily at the crowd as if searching for the reassuring presence of an old friend.

You mean Mick Jagger, Keith Richards? said Harry.

Keith Richards, bad teeth but great guitar sound, said Lenny. He is hero to all Polish musicians. Rolling Stones music is good for funerals, and birthdays too.

Lenny turned his back to the audience and chatted to the drummer. In Polish. Could they be talking about Keith Richards and his bad teeth? They bore the earnest look of dentistry students. Then Lenny leaned towards Harry, the accordion bulging on his chest and he was back in the 1950's and the accordion was a bus conductor's ticket machine. Make mine a single, Lenny, Harry was tempted to say.

I can't get no satisfaction, said Lenny. Rolling Stones. We play it, like devils.

He moved up to the mike, stuck a hand on his hip and squeezed out the opening chords of 'Satisfaction'. The drummer started to play, a clip-clop rhythm and the double-bass player was hanging over the neck of his instrument and bobbing his head in time to Lenny's version of the old Stones classic.

It sounded like a waltz to Harry's ears but what did he know, and he joined in with a breezy guitar line, trying to follow the beat of the original as faithfully as he could. Some of the audience clapped along, faces wrinkled and knees pressed together.

Da, da, dada-da, baba, boom-boom, sang Lenny.

One lively old dear pulled a plump little Polish fellow onto the floor. Her little feet flipping like windscreen wipers. Shots of vodka were repeatedly drunk as Lenny rambled on, the Polska Dots' version of 'Satisfaction' staggering to a halt with a demonic crash of cymbals. Lenny took a bow, inviting the crowd's approval, the drummer twirling his sticks in the air, making up for what he lacked in rhythm with a touch of showmanship. The double-bassist bowed with typical modesty. Some women were weeping. Lenny patted Harry's shoulder, and whispered,

I have no fear of death.

This is a special song for Lena, said Lenny, and silently he mouthed 'Happy Birthday to You' and Harry let go a huge sigh of relief.

He knew the song and could play along with the band but the next thing he knew there was a terrible thump and a scream from the crowd. Lena had collapsed to the floor. Harry could see Sylvester and Katy standing anxiously over Lena's stricken form and there were gasps and shrieks from people near to where she had fallen.

Lenny lay down his accordion. The bass-player frowned. The drummer smashed a cymbal.

The ambulance arrived with a stretcher in no time, a young man, and a young woman in green uniforms. They lifted Lena onto the gurney, still conscious, her head sticky with sweat, Sylvester shooing away the nosier guests from around the gurney and helping to form a free passage out of the hall.

So cruel for God to take her on her birthday too, said a woman's scratchy voice.

He is working overtime tonight that's for sure, said another voice, a man this time.

I heard that, said Lena. It is true. God is working at weekends. Overtime. Giving me a death on my birthday. What a present!

Lady, you'll be alright, don't talk so much, said the young woman from the ambulance team.

Harry had joined them from the stage and was standing beside the stretcher, his guitar slung half-way over his shoulder. Katy was there too, fearing her mother had suffered a stroke.

Are you the lady's relatives? asked the young ambulance man.

I'm her daughter, Katy Wackowski and this is Harry, my boyfriend, said Katy.

They were about to lift Lena into the back of the ambulance.

Would you care to join her on the short journey to the hospital? asked the young woman.

111

Katy and Harry climbed into the ambulance's rear, Katy taking hold of her mother's hand.

The food, there will be no food left now that I am gone, said Lena. Vultures!

Mother, said Katy, be still, you heard what the lady said.

Harry sat there, his guitar in his hands. Should he sing a song for Lena on her way to hospital in the ambulance? No one gave a performance in an ambulance. This was absurd and he felt guilty for thinking it possible. He placed the guitar on a chair and settled down. Lena was lying on her back, and Harry saw the crazy look had returned to her face. Katy's eyes flitted about the place before landing on her mother's face. Lena made to sit up, rising slowly, but exhausted by the effort she sank back to the gurney.

Mrs Wac-cock-ski, the ambulance lady said, smoothing out the thin blanket covering Lena.

Sorry, said Katy, it's Wack-ow-ski, not Wac-cock-ski

Mrs Wac-cock-ski, listen to your daughter.

Mum, said Katy, stay still, please. You will be alright.

The dying they look at you, said Lena. They look into your eyes because the essence of what they have left is inside you.

KERRY LYONS

Seventeen Weeks

Bianca can't remember when she last changed the bedsheets. Months ago, she decides. Maybe more. It's March now, and she's grown used to their tackiness, to the aroma of stale sweat and sleep. Clean sheets would signal some kind of surrender.

The sunlight slips through the cracks in the blind and flickers on the bedroom wall. *There is a whole world between discomfort and desolation*, she thinks. *A whole, other world.*

Bianca always assumed that her body would notify her within days of falling pregnant. Wasn't that part of being a woman? Recognising the signs? By the time she peed on the little stick and it came back with two pink lines instead of one, she was already nine weeks and two days. She and Karl were giddy with excitement and relief; no more scheduled coitus. They had struggled through a nine-month term of duty to achieve the second pink line. She was glad it was over, truth be told. They hadn't had sex since.

There may be some discomfort, the doctor had said. She knows now that he was deploying the word as a euphemism. The word comes from the Greek *eu* and *phēmē,* meaning "well" and "speaking". Well speaking. Or speaking well. Or speaking from the bottom of a well where the water is ice-cold and your voice disappears before it breaks the surface.

Skin is a surface too, Bianca thinks. The nuchal fold is a small fold of skin at the back of an unborn baby's neck housing a collection of fluid. It is of little interest in general terms but is important as a potential marker of abnormality in a foetus. Bianca perceives of abnormality as a sliding scale, a spectrum which begins at *unusual* and works its way down through *atypical*, *irregular* and *divergent* until it settles in the dust of darker words like *warped*, and *aberrant,* and *deviant.*

Light exists on a spectrum. If you follow visible light far enough, it will lead you into the bruised heartland of the gamma ray. According to cosmologists, gamma rays are spawned from violence. They are the children of dying stars, of solar eruptions, of the accretion which occurs when material is consumed by a black hole. Falling through the event horizon, Stephen Hawking suggests, is a bit like going over Niagara Falls in a canoe. The closer you get to the edge, the harder it becomes to resist the pull of the rushing water. Once gone, you will never resurface. Not in the same way, anyway, and not in the same universe, Bianca thinks.

On March 29, 1848, Niagara Falls froze entirely. Both the river and the falls were transformed into solid ice. It is the only time in recorded history that this has happened. Today is March 29. No wonder she feels so cold. Each day bears the scars of the days that have come before, and some days are colder than others.

Bianca checks the temperature on her phone. It is currently sixteen degrees in Blackheath, but the forecast suggests a high of nineteen by mid-afternoon. Autumn is still in its infancy in the mountains. She has always loved this time of year, but now there is an ache in her bones which refuses to go away.

Bianca remembers the coldest places she has ever been. Stonehenge in the middle of winter, where the dampness rose from the ground like a curse. The Skoftfell ice cave, where she imagined she was walking through the womb of winter itself. The Catholic church in Katoomba, where icy judgement sucked the warmth from her childhood in hour-long bursts.

The interior of the church was dim, and her winter breath would mist as she recited the lines. In summer, the heat would gather at the stone threshold but could never quite muster the courage to cross it. The wooden floor was frigid beneath her toes as she angled them over the soles of her sandals.

They were always late. Her mother had devised an arbitrary cut off to account for their lack of punctuality. If they managed to sneak into the church before the priest had finished his homily, then it counted as having attended the mass. If they arrived after the liturgy of the Eucharist had begun, then they had to wait for the next mass. Bianca remembers the sensation of her knees on the kneeler, bone on wood. Her covert shuffling to relieve her discomfort, followed by the whispered admonishments of her mother.

She hasn't set foot in a church for years, aside from weddings and funerals, and they don't count. There is a category outside of worship Bianca classifies as unavoidable obligation. Apparently, some parents hold a funeral service after the birth. The coffin must be the size of a shoebox, she thinks, or even smaller. Perhaps desolation is a rectangular prism.

The word prism comes from the Greek *prisma*, meaning "things sawn", or "sawdust", the particles left behind once something has been divided in two. Sawing is gradual process, rather than an instant severing. Pregnancy is gradual too, she thinks. Sawdust is potentially carcinogenic if inhaled.

It is safe to saw a piece of wood in two, Bianca understands, just as long as you remember not to breathe at the same time.

A baby born at seventeen weeks cannot survive outside the womb. Although the lungs have flowered inside the chest cavity, they are not yet ready to inflate. Breathing is an impossibility. Once the umbilical cord is cut, all oxygen supply is lost. The human brain can survive for around six minutes without oxygen. Six minutes is approximately the time it takes to make a cup of tea, inclusive of boiling the kettle, Bianca calculates.

On her left arm, she can still trace the faint outline of a childhood scar in the shape of a bear. She has another on her stomach, which is roughly the shape of Iceland. She has heard the story repeated so many times that she can tell it herself now, despite having no memory of the actual event. As she runs her finger down the bear's back, Bianca considers the exhaustion and failure that underwrite its history.

In simple terms, it is the story of a kettle sitting on a kitchen bench and the moment when it is accidentally upturned. The boiling water splashes out violently as the toddler plays on the floor near her mother's feet. There is a brief moment of silence before their screams merge in the drab kitchenette.

The young doctor who lives upstairs appears at the front door, having heard the commotion below. He runs a cold bath for Bianca, singing softly to calm her as she watches her skin inflate like a balloon. Half an hour later he lifts her small, shivering body from the water. It is the middle of July. He pats her dry with gentle hands before methodically salving and dressing her wounds. If the story were hers, she imagines that she would remember the sound of her mother's weeping, but it is not, and instead she remembers nothing.

The verb *disremember* is a colloquialism from the nineteenth century. It suggests the reverse engineering of memory, followed by the deliberate removal of unnecessary information from the brain. The verb *forget*, in comparison, suggests inadvertent neglect, or a simple failure to remember. Bianca picks at a thread which is beginning to break free from the old woollen blanket covering her thighs. She wonders if it is worse to forget your past, or to disremember it, and whether remembering is ever really a matter of choice.

The river Lethe, also known as the river of forgetfulness, flowed through the Underworld. Dead souls would drink from Lethe in order to forget all they knew and be born again through reincarnation. Nearby lay a spring named Mnemosyne. Souls who drank its waters would remember everything, gaining them entry to the Elysian Fields where they would enjoy eternal peace and happiness. Bianca does not understand how remembering everything could be perceived as a path to eternal happiness. Some things, she suspects, are best forgotten.

She was sitting on her bed when the call came from Dr Wilson. *I've just received the results from your twelve-week screening test*, he said. *I'm afraid they are not as good as we would hope. According to the tests, there is a one in twenty chance that your baby has a genetic abnormality such as Down syndrome. As a general rule, if the figures come back with anything under one in three hundred, I would recommend an amniocentesis. It is a simple procedure, with a very small risk of miscarriage. It can tell us for certain if there is an abnormality. I would urge you not to worry, there is every chance that your baby will be perfectly normal.*

A one in twenty chance isn't that bad, Karl pointed out that evening.

It's not that good, either, she replied.

You need to look at it the other way around. In nineteen out of twenty cases, everything will be fine. That's pretty good odds really.

Three weeks later Bianca lay on a narrow bed with crisp white sheets for the second time in a month. The room was small and dark, and the ceiling pressed down upon her. The light from the computer monitor emitted a cool glow. The doctor prepared a long, thin needle to insert through her belly and into her uterus. He needed to collect a small sample of amniotic fluid for further testing. Bianca felt her breathing grow ragged as she imagined the visceral sensation of metal through flesh. When the needle actually did pierce the surface of her skin, she was surprised by the lack of pain. There was a slight tugging sensation at the point of entry, a momentary discomfort, and then it was over. The results would take forty-eight hours. Total bed rest would reduce the chance of a miscarriage.

Bianca called the university and arranged for two days of sick leave. She hadn't provided notification of her pregnancy yet, so she told human resources that she had the flu. It seemed simpler than telling the truth.

The second phone call echoed the first. *I've just received the results from your amniocentesis. I'm afraid that the news isn't good. According to the tests, there is evidence of trisomy. You and Karl must decide whether you wish to continue with the pregnancy or terminate it. I'm afraid I can't make the decision for you. Only the two of you can decide. I can, however, tell you that in my experience most people in your position would choose to terminate. You have every chance of subsequent pregnancies being completely normal.*

The phone slipped from Bianca's hand. She watched impassively as Karl grabbed it from the quilt and put it to his ear. *Hi Graeme, it's Karl. Yes, yes, I understand. And there can be no error? Well, it is what it is, I guess. We'll decide by Tuesday. Absolutely, couldn't agree more. Thank you for calling. We'll see you then.*

The word terminate comes from the Latin *terminare,* meaning "to mark the end or boundary". Bianca finds it difficult to reconcile the concept of a boundary with that of an ending. The word *boundary* suggests that there is something lying beyond a defined perimeter, whereas the word *end* suggests a full stop with nothing to follow.

We need to talk about it, Karl told her after the telephone call. *You can't just shut down and refuse to talk to me. It's our baby, remember. I'm as upset as you are.*

In ancient times, the sea monsters Scylla and Charybdis lived on opposing sides of the Strait of Messina. Scylla had six heads and twelve feet. Her home was a shadow-filled cave high in one of the cliffs flanking the strait. As ships attempted to sail past, she would pluck unfortunate sailors from their decks and devour them. Charybdis took the form of a maelstrom, destroying any ships that strayed into her swirling waters. Sailors needing to traverse the strait were faced with an impossible choice. It was too narrow to avoid both monsters.

After a conversation in which Karl spoke frequently, and with unassailable logic, they came to the decision that Scylla was a better option than Charybdis. He argued that a certain amount of collateral damage was preferable to guaranteed destruction. If they continued with the pregnancy, they would face a lifetime of caring for an offspring with high needs. It may preclude them from having other children as they would no longer have the time, energy, or money. It may not be possible for them both to work, as their child would most likely require full-time care. And what kind of life would their child have in the end, anyway? What kind of life would they have?

When they arrived at the hospital on the day of the abortion, they found themselves directed to one of the birthing suites. Bianca had not considered that her moment of desolation would happen in parallel to someone else's moment of joy. It was an uncomfortable realisation. A woman screamed in the room next door and a newborn howled at the indignity of its arrival. Karl squeezed her hand as she sat down on the edge of the bed. *It would be more sensible,* she thought, *to carry out the terminations in a different wing of the hospital.*

The room was cavernous and the walls were painted institutional green. Bianca looked the colour up on her phone to pass the time while they waited for Dr Wilson to arrive. Its hex code was #B3CC99. Years ago, it was believed to have a calming effect on humans, but more recent research had debunked this myth. She tried to come up with a more appropriate colour but couldn't think of one she found calming enough.

Dr Wilson strode into the room. He was close to retirement age, with a face pitted and cragged from broken sleep. His grey hair was in a state of disarray, and there was a food stain on his collar. *Sorry to keep you waiting.* Bianca watched him rummage through a cupboard, grabbing items and dumping them into a plastic tray sitting atop a metal trolley. He wheeled it over to her bedside and pulled on a pair of blue nitrile gloves.

The prostaglandin gel will mimic your body's natural hormones, he explained. *If everything goes according to plan, we'll trick it into thinking that it's time to have the baby.* He squeezed a dollop onto his index finger. She spread her legs obligingly and the gloved finger slid inside her. The gel felt cold on the walls of her vagina. She stared out the window as Dr Wilson's finger gently circled. When he withdrew, she was acutely aware of the negative space, of the hollow that was left by his absence.

She was already seventeen weeks pregnant, so the safest method of termination was to induce labour. *You'll experience contractions and your cervix will dilate, just like in a normal labour*, he explained. *Obviously, your foetus is far smaller than a full-term baby, so the final phase will be much easier.* He patted her shoulder. *Try to get some rest now. It is unlikely that anything will happen before morning.*

To *induce* is "to lead by persuasion or other influences". Bianca shifted uncomfortably on the plastic-lined mattress and wondered if she had been too easily led. She considered all the words that had brought her to this point, but they were elusive now. Karl asked her how she was feeling. She smiled weakly but couldn't bring herself to speak.

When the contractions finally started about thirteen hours later, Bianca was grateful for the pain. She had barely slept, and anything was better than the waiting. She remembered being introduced to the concept of purgatory as a child. A place dedicated to the process of waiting. Not as bad as hell apparently, because it still held the possibility of redemption, but not too far off. Exactly how waiting led to redemption had never been made clear to her.

With each contraction, Bianca searched for a rhythm inside the pain. She hadn't attended any birthing classes. It was too early in the pregnancy for that. They didn't offer them prior to abortions, so she had no idea what she should be doing. At each consecutive tightening of her belly, she found herself foetal on the bed. Karl tried to stroke her hair, but she pushed him away. There was no comfort in his touch. Between each bout of pain, she barely had time to uncurl before she had to do it all over again.

She lost all sense of time in the room with the dirty green walls. Karl had fallen asleep in the chair next to the bed. They hadn't spoken for hours. The next contraction was the strongest yet, and she writhed on the bed, clawing the pillow for support. Dr Wilson materialised out of nowhere to check her progress. She tried to spread her legs, but they were shaking too much to oblige. He spread them for her with firm hands and slid his finger inside her again.

It's time, he said. *When the next contraction comes, I want you to push. When it stops, you stop pushing. Only push with each contraction. And remember to breathe. It will all be over soon.* He patted her shoulder. Karl had woken up and reached for her hand. She had no time to respond because another contraction was bearing down upon her.

Push comes from the Latin *pulsare*, meaning "beat" or "strike". There is a brutality to the word that Bianca finds apt. It is the repetition of pain that is depleting, she thinks, the knowledge that it will never stop, that it will only ever begin again.

There were twenty-three days between finding out she was pregnant and discovering that there may be something wrong with the baby. The word *wrong* comes from the Old Norse *rangr*, meaning "crooked". To be wrong is to lack straightness, to have deviated from the designated path.

Bianca had imagined having a baby prior to her pregnancy. She had envisaged how it would feel for her abdominal wall to stretch to breaking point, her muscles unknitting themselves to make room for a child. She had visualised her skin pulling taut, and then being rent asunder so her baby's head could emerge into the world. She had dreamt of a mouse squeezing through a hole only six millimetres in diameter.

When the next contraction came, she pushed down with her abdominal wall and felt a soft warmth enter her vaginal cavity. *Almost there*, Dr Wilson said. *One more push should do it.* As the wave of pain ran through her, she pushed again and something small and pliable slithered out of her. There was no searing pain, no stretching, just a formless slippage.

Hours later, Bianca searched for *foetal bone formation* on her phone. By thirteen weeks, she discovered, a baby has arms and legs, and well-defined fingers and toes. The basic skeleton is in place but is still formed from flexible cartilage. A process of ossification will occur over the next few months to harden and strengthen the bones. In the case of her baby, the process had not yet finished.

Bianca tried to disremember the slippery sensation from a moment ago, but it was impossible to forget. Dr Wilson tugged gently on the umbilical cord and asked her to push again. They still needed to birth the placenta. *If the placenta doesn't come, we'll need to take you to theatre to clear it out.* She pushed hard and the placenta was warm and gelatinous as it emerged between her thighs, an echo of the previous sensation.

119

Good work, said Dr Wilson.

The midwife finished swaddling her baby in a blue and white hospital blanket. A little mop of fuzzy black hair crowned a head about the size of a ping pong ball. He was small enough to fit in the palm of her hand. The midwife held him out. Bianca hesitated. It seemed wrong to grieve for an ending she had chosen.

Sometimes holding your baby can help you cope with the grief, the midwife said gently. There was an Irish lilt to her voice which Bianca found soothing.

She reached out to take him. He was soft and warm, and too small to be real. She breathed him in, knowing that this would be the only moment she would ever have to hold him. Reluctantly, she offered him to Karl, who shook his head. *I can't.* Bianca didn't argue. She placed a kiss on his tiny head and returned him to the midwife.

There was paperwork to be done and forms to sign. All deaths provoke a certain level of bureaucracy, even for those that have never really lived. Bianca's thighs were stained red, her muscles limp with fatigue. She was grateful when Karl stepped in to oversee the final administration. *No, they wouldn't be having a funeral. Yes, they were happy for the hospital to respectfully dispose of the corpse. No, a spiritual guide would not be necessary. No, they didn't require a plaster cast of their baby's feet or hands.*

Once it was all over, and their dead son had been taken away to wherever the aborted babies went, she lay back on the bed and closed her eyes. She heard Karl sink down into the armchair next to the bed and listened to his breathing gradually grow heavier. She had no desire to talk about what had happened. She just wanted to sink so deep inside herself that she would never find the surface again.

Bianca understands that there is a cold-eyed strength to be found at the core of grief, but she doesn't believe that she'll ever make it to the centre. The world feels hollow, and although she knows that there is solid metal at its heart, she also knows that she can never get there. To do so, she would have to traverse the molten outer core, and it is impossible to survive in lava.

Outside, Bianca hears the erratic pedalling of a child's tricycle on the footpath, and the finches chirruping in the eaves. She hears the level crossing sounding in the distance and knows that soon Karl's key will slide into the lock. Dust has begun to colonise the space underneath the old chest of drawers, and piles of books teeter on the bedside table. She crawls into the tangle of bedding and draws her knees up to her chest. Behind her eyelids she can just make out the red glow of the afternoon sun.

Alice

I hadn't seen or heard from Alice in months when she called me at two in the morning one Sunday in late June. She'd quit school earlier in the year to sing full-time for Carpet in the Jacks, a cover band her twenty-eight-year-old boyfriend Wayne co-founded with a cousin of his.

'Did I wake you?' she said.

'Yes.'

'It's Saturday night, you sad bastard.'

I was to be up early to go running with my girlfriend. Her family was big into running and I was trying not to hate it.

'Where are you?' I could hear a party in the background, muffled as though she was in a room away from it.

'Back at some gaff.'

'Snooping in some bedroom?'

She laughed. 'You know me too well.'

'I thought I didn't understand you, never did, never would?'

'Knowing and understanding are two different things.' I heard the rattle of ice in her glass. 'Can we forget the postmortem? It's annoying to have someone regurgitate things you said in an argument and use them as weapons against you.'

'Because you never do that.'

'Well, I'm different now.'

'Different how?'

'Will you pick me up?'

'Fuck, no.'

'Don't be like that. Please?'

'No.'

'Come on, don't be a prick.'

'Alice, I'm not picking you up. Get a taxi.'

'I've no money.'

'Where's Wayne?'

'He's fucking dead to me.'

'You broke up?'

'Just get me. There's some creep here who keeps following me. I can't tell if he's a predator or a bit special.

'Alice, I'm not picking you up.'

'I swear to fuck Ian, if you don't pick me up, and I mean this, I'll never speak to you again.' She hung up.

She sent me a pin drop to the address. Then a message that read, 'please, I need to see you x.'

I pushed open the door of my mother's bedroom. She was asleep. The television was on. After my father died, she was never able to drift off without it.

She usually kept the keys to her Civic on her locker. They weren't there. I searched in the pockets of her dressing gown. I found damp, balled-up tissues, one of my father's mass cards, but no keys. I turned off the television and went downstairs.

My sister Claire and her boyfriend were asleep on the couch. The end credits to *Apocalypse Now* were rolling. Claire's tit was hanging outside her string vest. Never great to see that.

I spotted the keys on the coffee table, glinting among the dozen beer bottles. Grabbing the keys, I knocked over two empties.

'What are you doing, creep?' Claire said.

'Nothing.'

She saw the keys in my hand.

'Where are you going?'

'Nowhere.'

'Don't tell me you're picking her up from somewhere?'

'Don't concern yourself.'

'You're a sad fuck.'

'Your tit is hanging out.'

'Fuck off, you absolute creep.'

I parked a few doors down from the house. I could hear music and voices coming from the back of it. I called Alice. Her phone rang out.

A seven-seater taxi pulled up outside the house and unloaded a group of lads and girls. With bags of cans, they made their way up the garden, giddy and laughing. The clock on the dash read 3.15.

I called Alice again and she answered.

'I'm outside,' I said.

'Come in,' she said.

'Alice!'

'Come in for five minutes and then we'll go, I swear.'

'You asked me to pick you up. I'm not going in there.'

She sighed. 'Fine, I'll be out now.'

Ten minutes later she came out of the house with some bloke. He was tall and wore his hair in a topknot. They hurried towards the car. She was carrying two bottles of vodka.

'This is Carl,' she said, getting in the front. 'Can you give him a lift?'

'What? No.'

Carl jumped in the back.

'Don't be like that,' she said. 'Carl's one of our own.'

'A hundred percent, man,' Carl said.

'You better drive, Ian,' Alice said, looking at the house.

Two lads had come to the front door. The taller one spotted us and shouted, 'Here!'

'Drive, Ian, for fuck's sake.'

The tall one ran out of the gate as I drove past. He sprinted alongside the car for a second or two before giving the back door a good boot. He collapsed on the deck. In my rearview I saw his friend rush over to help him up before I turned a corner.

Carl and Alice were still laughing when I drove out of the estate onto the main road.

'What the fuck was that about?' I said.

'These,' Alice said, waving the two bottles of vodka.

'And this.' Carl said, holding up a bag of coke.

'That could've ended very fucking badly,' I said.

'But it didn't,' Alice said. She opened a bottle and guzzled. She offered it to me. I shook my head. She handed the bottle back to Carl.

Alice picked up the CD pouch from the dash and started flicking through them.

'You've such great taste, Ian,' she said. They were mostly her CDs. She put on Fleetwood Mac's *Rumours* and skipped to "Dreams". She rolled the window down and lit a smoke and sang along with Stevie Nicks.

'Where am I dropping him?' I said.

Alice shrugged. 'Where do you live, Carl?'

'I live in the night,' Carl said, snorting coke off a coin.

'Right on, brother,' Alice said. She twirled a finger at her temple to indicate Carl's insanity.

'How about the beach?' Carl said. 'I'd love to hear the ocean.'

'The Irish Sea,' I explained to Carl, 'is not an ocean.'

He looked at me in the rear-view. He had a handsome face, square and clean shaven. His eyes were dark. 'It's a figure of speech,' he said.

'Great idea!' Alice said.

'I'm not driving you to the fucking beach.'

'What's with the cursing?' She said.

'You asked me to pick you up, *you* up. Now you want me to bring you and him to the beach.'

'There's no need for profanity,' she said.

'Yeah, man,' Carl said. 'Wreckin the buzz.'

The tide was in and the waves rolled up the beach just shy of the boulders that squared in the car park. An off-duty taxi was parked in the far corner near the pier. It was a warm, still night. A thin band of cloud stretched across an almost full moon. We listened to *Rumours* with the windows down.

Alice passed me a joint. I hadn't smoked weed since I started going out with Jane. I took two tokes and passed it back to Carl.

'Is there a lovelier sound than waves breaking on a beach?' Alice said.

'A beautiful woman moaning softly in your ear,' Carl said.

Alice burst out laughing.

'What?' Carl said.

'Oh, Carl, you are a gem.'

Carl took this as a compliment. He sat back, spreading his arms across the tops of the seats. Then he had a brainwave. 'Let's go for a swim,' he said.

'I'm good.' I said.

'Come on we go for a swim.'

'I can't swim,' Alice said, which was a lie.

'I'll teach you,' Carl said.

'I'll watch you,' she said.

Carl sat there for a moment looking at the water.

'Fuck it,' he said, and got out of the car.

He leaned against one of the boulders and took off his boots and socks, then his shirt, then his jeans. He wasn't wearing underwear. Naked, he waded into the water, yelping as the waves splashed up his legs. Alice giggled.

'Another tulip,' I said.

'I like him,' she said, squinting against the smoke from her joint. 'And look at his bum.'

'What about Wayne?' I said.

'He can jump off a cliff for all I give a rat's.'

She reclined her seat back and closed her eyes. In the dim light of the car I could just make out the nick of scar above her lip. She got it when she was eleven. Her stepfather Richard had slapped her so hard he sent her crashing into her bedside locker. I saw it through the slats of her wardrobe where I was hiding. It was the Saturday my family moved to Griffith Park, the day I met Alice.

'So, you broke up?' I said.

'I'm bored talking about it.'

'Are you still in the band?'

'What did I just say?'

'I'll take that as a no.'

'Take it whatever way you like.'

The headlights of the taxi came on. It swung around and lit up the car for a second before driving away.

'How's Lady Jane?' Alice said.

'She's fine.'

'I heard you two jog now.'

'Who told you that?'

'Lisa Keogh said she saw you two out one morning. I think she was trying to make me jealous, the silly cunt.'

'Were you jealous?'

'HA.' She took a nip of vodka. 'Look at this thing.' Carl was thigh-deep in the water and laughing hysterically. He had his arms stretched out at his sides. I couldn't decide whether he looked like he wanted to be saved or sacrificed. He let himself flop into the water. Alice laughed.

'Are you going back to school?' I said.

'Nope.'

'What are you going to do?'

'I'm going to London to stay with my da. He said there's plenty of work for good singers over there.'

I held my tongue.

'I don't want a lecture,' she said.

'Did I say anything?'

'I know what you're thinking.' She opened one eye and smiled at me. 'You'll miss me, but you'll have Lady Jane to keep you company. You can both get 600 points in your Leaving Cert, go to Trinity and become doctors or lawyers or whatever and get married.'

'Or *we* could get married.' I said.

'We will, after you and Lady Jane get divorced. Your kids will hate me.'

I laughed.

'Dick's anniversary next week,' she said and sipped some vodka.

Two years ago her stepfather Richard was killed after a fall down the stairs. He'd been drinking, as usual. Alice and I were in the house when it happened.

'Do you ever think about it?' She said.

'Sometimes.'

'Yeah.' She was staring absently at Carl coming out of the water. 'Fuck em,' she said and took a gulp of vodka.

Carl came to her window, covering himself with his bundled clothes. He was shivering and you could see his breath in the air. 'Are you coming in? It's so fucking cold. It's beautiful.'

'Not now, Carl, honey. Get back in the car.'

'Dryshites,' he said, and sat in the back seat and began the awkward task of putting his clothes back on. When he was done, he took a gulp of vodka and let out a loud whoop.

I got out of the car to take a piss. I inspected the back door where it had been kicked. There was no dent but there was a black streak. I rubbed at it and it disappeared. I walked over to the dunes. Beyond them, the sky was beginning to lighten.

When I got back to the car the two of them were kissing in the back seat. I sat down on a boulder and looked at the water. A flock of birds flew low and fast over the surface, their cries piercing the stillness of the morning. My sister was right: I was a sad fuck.

A sudden shout came from the car and then Alice screamed. I ran over and seeing him on top of her I opened the door. Alice was laughing. She had snagged one leg of her tights on something and it had torn away.

'Bit of privacy, here, man,' Carl said. 'Unless you want to join in.'

I closed the door and took a stroll up the beach. Why should I be so pissed off if we were just friends? I had a girlfriend for fuck's sake.

When I got back they were still at it. I sat back down on the boulder. It wasn't long after when I heard the door open. I turned around and saw Carl standing by the car, putting his t-shirt on. He winked when he saw me and walked over towards the dunnes.

I sat into the car. Alice was in the back, smoking.

'Well, that was a laugh,' she said.

I could see Carl in the rear-view pissing over by the dunes. He had his jeans down all the way to his ankles, like the way you piss when you're a kid.

'Are you not talking to me now?' Alice said.

I turned the key and started the engine. Carl looked around, a cigarette in his mouth. I put the car in gear and started driving.

'Hey,' he roared and started pulling up his trousers.

'What are you doing?' Alice said, laughing, turning around to look at Carl. He was sprinting with one hand holding up his jeans towards the entrance of the beach, trying to cut us off. I put the boot down.

'Alice,' he shouted. 'Stop!'

Alice

Alice giggled. She reached into the back and grabbed the unopened vodka bottle. She buzzed down the window.

'One for the road,' she shouted and tossed it onto the sand as we drove off the beach, leaving him stranded. I don't know about Alice but I hadn't laughed like that in a long time.

I parked a few doors down from her mother's house. We shared a joint. The morning sky was blue and cloudless. The clock on the dash read 6.10.

'I'm supposed to be up for a jog in an hour,' I said.

'No? With her Highness?'

'Yep.'

'Jesus wept, man. It must be love.'

She passed me the joint.

'What happened with Wayne?' I said.

'God, what is the obsession with Wayne?'

I shrugged.

'It's such a cliche, it's embarrassing,' she said. 'He was seeing this other singer behind my back, some bitch he used to be in a band with. So I fucked Liam our drummer and that was the end of Wayne, and the band.'

'And now you're going to London.'

'Now I'm going to London.'

I nodded.

'Will you miss me?' she said.

'You know I will.'

'I know.' She smiled at me. 'Me ma will be up soon with the twins. I want to be in bed before she is.'

'Tell her I was asking for her,' I said.

'She'll be glad to hear I was with you tonight.'

She kissed me on the lips and got out of the car. I watched her walk to her gate, one black tight intact, one bare leg. She lifted the lid of a neighbour's bin and tossed in the empty vodka bottle and disappeared into her house.

She left for London two weeks later. I didn't see her before she went and I haven't heard from her since.

1967

He was late and walked quickly pausing for an elderly man who muttered a repetitive dirge, one of the regulars of the street. Inside shafts of thin light filtered through the concourse; a strange constant to the noise and motion of the place. The sight of her gathered his insides. Joe watched as Anna made her way through the crowds of greetings and farewells standing aside, waiting for them to pass. Her English manner was evident at fifty paces. His own regard for others was borne of a different consideration. He wondered if they were just too damned considerate to survive.

'Hey baby, you okay?' He embraced her briefly while a short man in a baseball cap spat into the gutter at their feet.

'I'm fine, but thought I was going to miss the train. Beth was still in bed and there was no one around to look after Stella; she wasn't too happy about me leaving.'

'Who? Beth?'

'No, no... Beth's permanently happy, every night. Beats me how she gets up in the morning.'

'Doesn't sound like she does.'

'No... Stella wasn't happy. I guess she knows no one will be paying much attention. I wish I didn't have to leave her, not overnight.'

'Well, that's just too bad.'

They walked in silence too hot to touch. Her dress clung to her damp thighs in minutes. New York settled on her tongue, thick and odorous after the fresh breeze of the sea, and she turned away to suppress the tears that welled-up in a regular tide of anxious doubt. Joe placated, 'Don't worry, Stella will be fine. She's a tough cookie.'

'It's not that... What time are we due?'

'Later. Let's go and sweat it out at home. I need some shade.'

A rhombus of light fell through the open window onto the parquet. The radio was burbling in the corner, covering the baseball with the odd roar from a distant crowd. Anna dropped her bag and sprawled on the bed. 'Do you think anyone ever gets used to this heat?'

'Nope, those who can just leave.'

'You know, this whole place smells of you. It hit me when I came through the door... A sort of stale-man smell, slightly sharp.'

He sat down, frowning, and caressed her face, 'Stale?'

'No, I like it. But it's better fresh.' She burrowed her nose in his neck. 'You know, I think smell has a shape. Yours is decidedly round. A warm, round smell, then over time it becomes... a polygon.'

'You want to talk about it?'

'No, not particularly. What is there to talk about? Do we have a choice?'

Joe listened to the radio briefly before responding, 'You know what I think.'

'I can't take the risk. You know that Joe. You know what the lawyer said, if we have this child, I'll lose Stella...' She held his face in her palms, 'You know it.'

Anna hauled herself off the bed and lit the stove to make coffee. He followed, fetched a beer from the icebox and rolled the bottle along her forehead. 'You want one of these? It might make you feel better.'

'No, I've gone right off alcohol.'

'Did that happen the last time?'

'Pretty much. It's not uncommon. How long have we got?'

'Till nine, after dark. It's at one of the projects in Queens.' The kettle boiled, 'Jeez, that whistle, you'd think they'd alter the pitch, the sound gets right under my skin.'

Joe turned off the gas and filled the filter, while an oily slick spread across the black surface bright as a bird's wing,

'Like me, you mean?' Anna, took off her dress and returned to bed.

He smiled, 'Nothing like you, not like you at all... God, I've missed you.'

Joe ran his finger down the fine line from her navel, placed his dark hand over her pale belly and for a brief moment allowed himself to imagine the birth of their child. Lying behind her, his long body followed the contours of her own. A siren swelled and receded in the street below as the traffic gathered pace for rush hour. She sat up, 'You been getting any of your own work done?'

'Oh, I've been wading through molasses. Thoughts too slow to keep the script going. Perhaps when this is all over. How about you?'

'I painted a lurid sunset from the end of the jetty. You know, with a clutch of masts off-centre. It's up for sale at the marina, but I think I left in too much irony. You really have to believe in that sort of thing for it to work.'

129

'I guess.'

'Mostly I'm minding the children anyway. The youngest is a bit of a monster. It's tough being at the end of the line like that. His parents don't give him much time; Beth seems to have moved on and Bob has always been preoccupied.'

It was the right decision; there was no doubt about that; holding on to the idea was the problem. She thought of her daughter, thinning-down now and suddenly a child rather than a baby. The girl was impossibly pale like the father; on their first day in Sag Harbor her back had blistered badly. The memory made Anna feel guilty still. They had found a dead horseshoe crab, belly-up on the shore, the inside fine and delicate beneath the huge carapace. Clams squirted jets of salty water from below the sodden surface as they walked along the sand. She had made a net from an old cotton flour bag and Stella had caught a terrapin in the oily water of the marina.

Anna wondered what her former husband was doing. She couldn't imagine being with him now, the idea of him seemed vague, except for the constant motion. It was strange how quickly the sense of him had left her mind. In the summer the days seemed all alike, long and immobile punctuated by the occasional storm. It was hard to keep track of time under the weight of heat; but for the legacy of the child the marriage might never have happened. Joe got the old sock out from inside his boot at the back of the closet. He rolled up and inhaled deeply.

Anna's brow furrowed, 'It's a little early for that, don't you think?'

'Come on, girl. Cut me some slack, it's not like this day is normal.'

The light outside had dropped below the line of the street and the flickering sign from the drugstore cast a frenzied shadow on the wall above the bed. She felt like a bit-part in a bad movie, leaden as she rose to shower and dress. Joe sat in the gloom almost invisible against the curtains, but his long dark hand struck a tight rhythm against his knee revealing both his presence, and his state of mind. He looked up, 'I'll get the car, it's a few blocks away.'

'It's okay, we can walk together. I'd like to walk.'

The street sounds were muffled by the heavy air. Joe shortened his stride to match hers and they made the four blocks in silence. The sound of their steps was pronounced, like the click of cutlery during an awkward meal. Anna got a shock from the door handle of the car. She swore and continued, 'I got the papers for the custody case; it's next month, the 27th. My lawyer says I should be available, but probably won't have to attend. You know what else he said... We can come back when it's over, but I can't risk bringing Stella to the City before then.'

'I can't wait for it to be over.'

The car was beat-up, but after clearing its throat for a few minutes it kicked-in. They pulled out, rocking over the holes in the road. Joe said, 'It's quite a way, and then when you get to these places it's almost impossible to find the entrance.'

He looked over, 'You've probably never been to a project before.'

They drove through the enclosed space of Riverside Drive. She could hear the metal jangling inside the tyres, bouncing off the shuttered concrete and waited for relief. Joe continued, 'She's retired now, of course. Rick said not to use our names. No introductions, just to say that he sent us.'

'How's the show going?'

'Good. Very good; it looks set to become a cult.'

'I've never liked musicals.'

'Each to his own, hey baby? Anyhow, musicals is how we got the contact. All those showgirls getting into trouble; Rick knows all about them.'

'But after Stella, I should have known better.'

'It's easy to say. I think I just willed it too much. I sure am sorry either way.'

The City spread out in vague uniformity; blocks of patterned light broke the dark horizon and the car lurched over the broken surface of the road. Joe tuned-in for the ball-game results. He smiled, 'Now there's something to smile about.'

'What?'

'The baseball. We're still in with a chance.'

'Oh, that. I can never care who wins; it's nothing to do with me, with us.'

Joe took his hands off the wheel and extended his arms. 'That's the whole point really. It's a small, bright space outside all of this stuff.'

'I'd have thought you'd switch allegiance since you made a place for yourself here.'

'Hey, you never desert your home team... And now they're doing real good. And I do care, I really do.'

They were quiet for a while, until he noticed her clenched jaw and peeled eyes.

'Oh Anna, don't… I didn't mean to put pressure on you. We've made the decision. I'm sure it's right, hang on to that. You know, you think about a thing and you form an opinion and then you don't have to think about it anymore. You've done all your thinking on this one. We both have.'

'I'm so frightened. Throwing one away to keep the other. Being told by your lawyer to break the law. It's crazy.'

'I know, I know. We just have this thing to do and then it's all over. No more thinking.'

They drove on through the blank streets. The heat never let up, even in the night it was thick and palpable. Dark stains spread across the surface of the road where the hydrants had been let off and groups of youth gathered beneath the few that were still going. Drops of water glistened in the colour of the adjacent signs and a rosy glow bloomed on the growing pools. Store windows were boarded-up or held dusty displays; two hubcaps and a ball of string, a pair of boots and a cardboard cut-out of Santa Claus with a bottle of Coke. Joe pulled over to check the map and a young girl in hot pants leaned into the window. Anna looked down, embarrassed, as the huge cleavage fell into the car, 'You guys want to get there with me?'

'Hey, back off, okay?'

'Just trying to do my job.'

'Well do it someplace else.'

Joe pulled out and turned left at the next corner. In front was a huge lot. Ranks of cars were herded into a regular grid with oil spills grouped in the centre of those that were empty. They got as close to the building as they could and parked.

'You ready?'

Anna nodded.

'Now we just have to find a way in.'

They got out and walked round the base of the huge block. Graffiti made its way up the walls; *Yankees* was scrawled in the appropriate typeface, along with the usual raised fists and messages of love. Litter tumbled along the sidewalk, blown into brief spirals by the warm wind which had gathered pace on the journey.

'Feels like a storm's coming.'

'Is that a good omen, or bad?'

'I don't know about omens, but it would sure clear the air. Most times they just seem to pass us over, one big empty promise.'

Inside the brutal light revealed the fatigue on Anna's face. Joe smoothed her hair. The entrance hall was dispossessed, untended and unloved. She felt herself slipping away; all her private delights pressed under the weight of this reduced reality.

'How do you hold on to yourself in such a place?'

Joe inclined his head, 'I don't know. God or drugs, or both. A lot of people don't.'

She indicated the graffiti on the walls with a sweep of her arm, 'Think I would have to do a whole self-portrait. Twice.'

The elevator stank. Ascending ponderously to the fourteenth floor, it shuddered like an overloaded weightlifter. Joe knocked and waited while they were examined through the fish-eye. The door opened and a black guy in his sixties stood before them. The expression on his face was blank. He had a pale vest over his taut belly and a dark stain of sweat flowed down to his navel. There was no greeting. Joe said, 'Rick sent us.'

'You'd better c'mon in then.'

The apartment was dim and the blue light from the television trawled the walls. Everything was lace and bows; pretty, sweet, cheap. Joe squeezed Anna's hand and sat down on the sofa with the old guy and the television, as an old woman came through the door at the back. She pointed at Anna and said, 'You can come on through now.'

Anna followed through to a rear bedroom. The light was bright, and faded photographs of brief childhoods were lined up on the window sills. The woman was small and darker than her husband. She clacked around in fluffy, pink mules with her heels spread under the weight of years. Anna suppressed a nervous urge to laugh. Here was an urban gothic. There would be no comfort, no communion. This was business. The woman turned to the dressing table and said, 'You can take off your things now and lie on the bed.'

She used a catheter. The pain was precise, but bearable. She said nothing would happen for about twenty-four hours, and left the room. Anna dressed and caught three versions of herself reflected in the dressing-table mirror.

Joe placed an envelope on the corner of the low table as they left. In the corridor he held her shoulders and studied her face. 'You okay?'

Anna nodded, and whimpered quietly, 'Oh Joe, she disapproved of me, of us. She's thinking I wouldn't have the baby because you're black, right?'

'Shh, no, she was just trying to keep herself to herself. She didn't want to get involved is all. It's her job, you'll never see her again, what does it matter? C'mon, no more thinking now, I told you.'

They left for the station early the next morning and walked to Grand Central as the day warmed into life. There had been rain in the night and the city sounds spread away over the buildings, buoyant on the expanding air. When they reached the concourse Joe turned and held her shoulders, 'You call me, okay? And if there are any problems go to the doctor right away, you hear?'

She nodded, and felt very small. Childhood lasted for such a short time. Sometimes she wished her own had lasted a little bit longer, for the lack of awareness of her troublesome body, the lack of desire for anyone else's. They embraced in a quiet corner, and she had time to memorise the deep fillets that ran down his back, splaying to the shoulder blades. Joe removed her hands, and held them in his pale palms. Their fingers entwined. There were perfect moons on his nails. They parted and he left quickly without looking back.

Stella was in the pool when she got back, crashing about in a yellow T-shirt; a scrawny, fearless, white thing. The coils of red hair were momentarily smoothed flat by the water, so long when wet. On seeing her mother she shouted, 'Mommy!' and clambered out, stubbing her toe on the side and hopping the remaining two steps, desperate to offer a wet hug.

'I can swim a length and I lost my shoes, the sea took them from the shore. Look.'

The child jumped in and clambered a length, spluttering. It was an effort of will more than anything else.

Smiling Anna said, 'That's great honey. I'm going to find Beth.'

'She's not feeling very well. She's inside.'

Anna entered the gloom, 'Beth?'

'Hey you, did it go okay? Are you alright?'

Beth looked grey. The ashtray was already full.

'Yes. I think I'm fine. But I may need to go to the doctor later, just for a check-up.'

Beth sat up and lit another cigarette, 'Use mine, he's cool.' She groped around the kitchen counter for her address book. Her hand was shaking, 'Here's the number.'

'Thanks. You don't look so good.'

'Too many parties, and I'm getting too old, but Bob just keeps on going and I just keep up, 'Just' being the operative word.'

'Where are the children?'

'They've gone to the marina to get ice-cream. The youngest was having a tantrum. They should be back any minute.'

'Well, I'm here now, if you want to go back to bed.'

'I might do just that.'

It started that evening in a steady flow, both the blood and the tears. Stella had fallen fast asleep, knocked out by the sun and the sea air. Anna poured herself a whisky, but it tasted harsh and alien. She sat alone in the beach-hut blubbing for a time, and then blundered through to watch her sleeping child with the huge freckles on her wide, lash-less face. It was a decision, like any other; she could let it screw her up, or she could keep it together. She slept with the light on.

The appointment was late the next afternoon. She left Stella with Beth and walked across the bridge into town. The doctor was clean, with manicured nails and a certain fastidiousness to his manner she found unattractive. He had the smooth symmetrical features of a happy childhood; no scars, no shortage of food, no chemical abuse, no insults, no deprivation whatsoever. But his face was open and generous. She soon relaxed and felt mean-spirited for damning his perfect teeth. He took her temperature and felt her belly, after asking about the flow. He then sat down and swivelled on his chair, 'Everything seems fine, absolutely fine.'

Anna stood up, 'It has been such a worry, the whole thing.'

'I'm sure, but it's done now, no time for regrets. Tell me, do you think it would be a suitable place for some of my other patients. It's something I'm asked for frequently. Very frequently in the summer months.'

'It's in Queens, you know?'

She tried to summon up the place with her expression, 'I don't think it would be appropriate. It wouldn't be appropriate at all.'

'That's fine. Shame. Anyhow, good luck. If you have any problems you know where I am.'

They shook hands, and she left, making a detour back along the beach, finding that line in the sand where all trace of footfall is lost to the water in minutes.

When Anna got back to the house, Beth was sitting at the kitchen counter smoking, she said, 'Well, that took a while, where have you been?'

'I'm sorry, I...'

'It doesn't matter. You're back now.' She stubbed out her cigarette, 'Things aren't so good Anna.'

It seemed the youngest had dropped a brick on the terrapin, killing it outright. Distraught Stella had stormed off somewhere, but not before using some terrible language. Beth was outraged, 'I don't care where she went, but if that brat can't learn to control her mouth in front of the little-one, I'll have to let you two go. I know we've become friends, Anna, but I have my own family to think about…'

'I'm so sorry. I'll go fetch Stella and tell her off.'

Anna kept her eyes down, contrite. She needed this place, just until the court case was over. 'I'll put them all to bed when I get back.'

Anna left and walked back towards the marina. She could see Stella at the end of the long jetty, shoeless, her red hair burning on the water. She watched as the child put the body of the terrapin into the cotton flour bag along with a stone weight, and struggled to tie the top with a piece of twine before throwing the bag into the sea. Stella then stood up, chest out proud, and gave a stiff salute, as the strange parcel turned in the water. Anna walked along the jetty and arrived just as it sank from view. The sun cast a long arm out across the sea and a cool breeze was gathering. Stella reached for her hand and burst into tears, 'Mommy, I don't cry when you're not here, because there isn't any point, but then when I see you I can't seem to help it.'

'I know.'

Anna stroked the flaming hair.

'But he killed my terrapin, it was my best thing. I was just showing it to him, and he dropped a brick on it. The little dumb-fuck.'

'I know that too. Beth is very sorry. But she's also upset, I would like you to apologise to her for swearing.'

'But he is a dumb-fuck.'

'I know he is. But he's young yet, he'll grow out of it one of these days. There's still no excuse for swearing.'

'But it makes you feel better.'

She smiled down at her strange, fiery daughter, 'I know'.

The whining rasp of a transistor radio meandered across the water. Anna paused to listen as Joe's team hit a home-run. 'We're going to win', she thought.

THOMAS O'MALLEY

Caravan

It was wind and war that forced them wide around the rim of the great sand sea. Days fell away under the slow plod. After the last sack of split peas was shaken inside out, only wild tamarisk kept the camels going. Four had already been thrown away, the life walked out of them. And there were many marches ahead.

With each camel that caved, kneeling in deference to the sun and the sky and the fathomless space, those that continued the forward sway bore the brunt. Loads were increased, so marches had to be cut short. The caravan crawled like a slow bug. What wells could be found were salted mires. More camels would drop, and then what? It was grim arithmetic, taking the long way around.

The men survived on millet flour, mutton fat and muttered curses. There were five. All steppe men. The Overseer. Furious and footsore, his pony too far gone to bear his bulk. And the four pullers. Old Oktai. Bold, the sneak. Tomor, with the torn ear. And Enebish. The runt. The pawn.

Howls of dust turned the sky to yellowed bone for days on end, and dyed the night blacker than old blood. So black that depressions were ruinous. A dry creek bed, in the dark, would snap with glee an overburdened leg. So they marched from pre-dawn to noon. Then off came the packs, two men to a camel, working up the lines. Up went the tent. On went the pot, over a fire of dung and brush.

Enebish. The runt. Given up by his father to the traders. And this his first run. Up against it. A fool in a world that feeds on fools. Far gone from the kinship of other caravans, from roving grain pedlars and good wells. Camels dropping like felled trees. But Enebish was young and hungry enough to chew through the hardships. The back-breaking loading and unloading. The cold nights. The lice. The lethargy. The debilitating challenge of walking slower than comes naturally for hours at a time. Here, on the brink, was manhood. Swiftly was learned the lot of a puller.

But what Enebish didn't know would fill a lake bed. His cohorts were heartless as carcasses. They were special kinds of scoundrels, even for traders. Their cargo of fleece and pelts a sham that swaddled wrappers of oily, reeking opium. They were dope runners, sharing nothing except an

137

oath to divide the take four ways on delivery. Enebish, the fool, number five, a fawn among wolves, would be thrown away when the time came.

In the tent, when the camels were turfed off to hunt thorns, and the pot was spent, they arranged their bedrolls according to rank. Enebish had the threshold, where the wind whipped and flapped and harried at his back like scolding hands. The Overseer chided Enebish for being a skinny cunt and letting the cold in. Bold, the sneak, the skinniest cunt of all, sniggered. Enebish laughed too, and felt a flicker of something. So this was camaraderie.

Routine was everyone's friend in the abyss. They set off each day in the pre-dawn murk, long ranks of camels, tethered nose to tail, padding into the void. Four trains in convoy, with the Overseer at the head, then Bold, Tomor, Oktai, and Enebish at the rear, leading their lines. No bells or demented dogs marked their progress. Theirs was a creep of soundless, soulless stealth. Day after day. Any sense of miles gained marked only by the listless sag of humps drained of fat. Their world was a black gravel desert, slate shards like shattered tiles, nature's endless war. The sun alone eyed their progress, but offered no comfort. It was a mere shape, small and diffuse, a button, suspended behind blanket billows of dust.

The road was the biggest scoundrel of all, tricking and hustling them off into salt bogs and shifting sand hollows. The camels would bunch up and bicker, forcing the Overseer to heft himself up a rise, or be hoisted on to the back of a camel. If the way could not be seen, steps were retraced, the cruellest outcome. Eventually, half a march wasted, one of the men would fix eyes upon an ovoo, a cairn of stones, entropy-defying, beauty from chaos, and proclaim that they were back on course. The Overseer would circle the ovoo three times, splashing imagined droplets like a holy man. On the final pass, with ritual solemnity, he would place a stone carefully among the others. Enebish watched each time with reverent exhilaration.

All mumbled oaths and finger flicks of flour, the dope-runners clung to pious superstition like infants to their mothers. When a camel was thrown away, it was beyond taboo to lay a finger on it. It must remain, unmolested, where it dropped, for all that their stomachs screamed for meat, lest the ghost of the beast trail them through the sands bringing calamity in its wake. Let the desert take what it wants, was the litany.

For days, the caravan inched across a vast crateral depression that tapped the life from their legs. At its nadir, the iris of that great sunken eye, a camel in Enebish's line unravelled from the inside out. Dread barks and devil wails alerted the others. Enebish stopped the train, in error. The Overseer, all fret and fear, whipped the quivering beasts moving again.

The cow had been in calf. The trick, he told Enebish, is never to let the camel see, and then it won't become attached and force a stop, refusing to move again. Enebish nodded, grateful for new wisdom. Eyes ahead, ever onwards. He didn't dare look back himself to see what had been left behind. Let the desert take what it wants.

Eyes ahead, to a hairlip of mountains that inched up and across the horizon by degrees, squaring with their line of approach. They were up on level ground again, and the road was bending at last. Somewhere beyond those distant decayed teeth was their destination. The rendezvous. The Overseer pushed his knife through the willing neck of his pony in celebration. The men watched and licked their lips as the bone-handled blade, beaming at its renewed usefulness, disassembled the pony into parts. Thick soup warmed their spirit and gave vigour to their spite. Enebish ate his fill of camaraderie that night and the next. And the next.

Enebish. The runt. For all the slow-motion misery, the camel stink, the aching hardships and dirty jibes, there was something else at play. An awakening. Call it the instinct of the leaf to bend towards the light. New perspectives formed like calluses. Boy muscles knotted like wood. Hard miles brought with them flickers of elation, even as the noose tightened. He watched the birth and death of a storm, a saga for the ages, as others snored. He saw antelopes, a herd of thousands, melt into the gloom like whispers.

Only once did he ask, in the fire-crackle quiet, his voice high and pure and reedy, how much longer their journey would take. It must have been yet another taboo because nobody said a word. For his mistake, Enebish pinched himself in the dark until tears cleaned his cheeks. The next day, The Overseer received his tea in bowed silence. Old Oktai, slow and desolate, wouldn't meet his eye as they worked up the line of camels, facing one another, heaving on that illicit, concealed cargo. In his misery, Enebish wished for a giant hook-beaked bird to swoop down and carry him away.

Bold alone broke silence and tempted the fates. He squatted at the fire, a coiled whip, picking his teeth with his knife and arrowing Enebish with wolf eyes. "Enebish", he said, slowly, pulling apart the name like bones. The name chosen by Enebish's grandmother to fool the demons. Demons that came in the night to snatch away first sons. 'Not this one', it meant. "Enebish".

For all that he tried, Enebish couldn't bring himself to love Bold like he loved The Overseer. Only Bold trampled him on his way out to piss. Only Bold kicked his tea across the dirt. Bold had something about him that made even Tomor and Oktai keep their distance. He was all sinew, limbs like bent branches, the muscled spider fingers of a strangler. He had a barbed tongue that made the others wince or grunt or cackle. Though it was seldom aimed at The Overseer, just like a son would never slander his own father.

The Overseer, at the head of the tent, furthest from the threshold, was father to them all, even to white-whiskered Oktai, because he knew most about the road and its secrets. Behind those bloodshot eyes, his mind was a hoard of omens and oaths and legends, the unwritten bylaws and protocols of the camel men passed up the line, tail-to-nose, from times forgotten. In a caravan, knowledge was all, and he was king, at his most stately when sat high up on a laden camel, or sprawled on his side sucking the stem of the opium pipe Enebish dutifully cradled for him, night after night, as he spoke his dreams in hushed breaths. The Overseer was, admirably, still fat even as Enebish felt his own clothes dropping loose.

Leaner still, though ineligible for pity, were the camels. After weeks rounding the hook of the great sand sea, they were now seven down, a crumb trail of collapse in the caravan's wake. Several more teetered on the wrong side of utility, and had to be cajoled and kicked, sometimes brutally, or hauled to their feet by all the men, working together, in order to continue the forward plod. At the fire, Enenbish listened to grave debates about burying cargo under the desert, should it come to it. The thought almost brought him to despair. The shame of coming up short on his first run was too much to stomach. He prayed, fists clenched, and promised the fates to do whatever was needed to succeed.

By some sliver of clemency, the dust that hounded them for weeks swallowed back its spite and melted into the earth. Their windless world was made new, brilliantly defined, a moonscape dappled by the shadows of buffeting clouds. But to Enebish it meant that loneliness was now existential in scope. As he trudged, leading rope over his shoulder, his eyes scanned the horizon for a little dome of white, a tell-tale rise of smoke, a pinprick of humanity, somewhere with a door and a stove and a heart.

They were, of course, lonely by design. Enebish understood that wind and war had forced them wide around the rim of the great sand sea. To the road untraveled. Sometimes, in the dark, as Enebish laid flame to The Overseer's pipe, he would be rewarded with sordid tales of bandit packs and their skinning knives, rogues and rustlers that travelled under cover of rival caravans, ambushes by mounted bullies shaking down traders for transit taxes in the name of some interim warlord. Enebish listened hungrily, a scavenger for wisdom, as the others dropped away into unconsciousness. The old trade routes, Enebish learned, even those mostly lost to neglect,

Caravan

were to be circumvented like a festering corpse. Instead, they were taking
their chance in no-man's land, the lesser of oblivions, where nobody dwelt
nor would follow, and playing their hand against nature instead.

But it happened that they were not alone. Even out on the unpeopled
brink, the caravan was being tailed. The pursuer began as a tiny dot of
doubt nagging at their rear – a wild camel? An ibex? A phantom? – and
grew into a rude brushstroke of panic. The Overseer called a halt to the
caravan. Tomor fished out a rust-worn carbine from the packs, raging at
his fumbling hands. Oktai hushed the twitchy camels with words. Enebish
picked up a stone and rotated it in his palm until he found his purchase.
They waited.

It took an age for the pursuer to get close enough for Tomor to have
half a chance of putting a bullet through him. By then, the listless pageant
of an old man, frail and frazzled as burnt paper, progressed in silent
ceremony. The camel he rode was a wreck of sores. A second camel, laden
with his worldly belongings, trailed behind. The man's umbilical beard
and alien cap marked him as a traveller from antique lands. The Overseer
stood them down. Down went Tomor's rifle, and Enebish's stone.

The old man was a pilgrim, he told them, in a tongue they couldn't
understand. He had been on the road for a month or a year or a lifetime.
He was on his way to a mountain, somewhere of godly importance to his
people, a quest of delusional ambition. With both hands clasped, he
bowed over and over, like a pecking hen. He hauled down his food stores
off the camel as offering, weevil-chewed grain spilling from a cloth bag
as the men watched. The implication was clear even though the words
were not. The old man wished to fall in with their caravan. To Enebish's
surprise, The Overseer agreed.

The old man proved a wellspring of usefulness. Around camp he
foraged more than his share of dung for the fire. He brewed tea and took
his last of all. He never made a sound, apart from the woodwind murmur
of prayer, nor did he lay a glance on their camels or cargo. On the third
day, he snared a fat marmot outside its hole, then cooked it by stuffing its
body with stones scorched in the fire. Enebish gnawed contentedly at a
fatty limb with little splayed toes, and felt nothing but gratitude and
admiration for The Overseer's fine judgement.

The arrival of the old man meant a promotion for Enebish, who moved
one clock space into the tent, away from the threshold. Once it was agreed
that the old man couldn't understand them, they cursed him with
impunity, mocking his habits, his odour, his gods. Every day, the old man
would find a flat rock to kneel on and worship at the sun. Sometimes he

did this on a march. Enebish would watch over his shoulder as the old man dwindled to a speck behind the rear of the train. Later he would make up the ground between them, always leaving a train's length between himself and Enebish at the rear of the caravan.

Once, the old man trotted up beside Enebish, dismounted from his camel and walked beside him. They didn't speak. The old man reached into his cloak and handed Enebish a little strip of dry meat. Enebish took it and popped it in his mouth. It tasted like salted leather. The old man smiled a three-tooth grin.

Some days later, as the caravan passed along a narrowing fissure like blood through a vein, he came alongside again. This time he gave Enebish a stone. A stone with a secret. It was cracked apart in two pieces like an egg, a galaxy of purple crystals revealed within. The old man grinned. And then he sang, his tremulous voice wavering between just two or three notes. Enebish listened to those indecipherable sounds, and wondered about the closeness of beauty and despair.

The next time the old man came alongside Enebish, he didn't smile, and he didn't sing, and he didn't offer anything. Instead he took his finger, crooked and sad, and drew it across his throat. That night, under stars so brilliant it was like you could sweep them all up in open arms, they murdered the old man.

Enebish dozed as The Overseer and Bold entered the tent, two children bursting with a delicious secret. The Overseer held an open skin of wine. He proclaimed that they were saluting the death of the old pilgrim, the end of his long journey. He was laid out on his back when they found him, he said, a mask of peaceful reverence on his face. And now he was with his ancestors, dancing the dance of the young and virile once again. The Overseer recalled all of this, eyes half-closed in sodden eulogy, while simultaneously trying to shield the wine away from Bold's snatching grasp. Oktai and Tomor cast down their eyes.

Enebish got to his feet. He wanted to leave the tent and gulp the air. Bold's talons shackled his wrists. The Overseer, now paternal and soppy stern, took Enebish aside. It was dreadful luck to whine at the grave of a pilgrim that dies on the road, he explained. He put an arm around Enebish, and gave him his first ever taste of wine. You're a man now, he said. And every man's journey ends in death, one way or another. Let the desert take what it wants.

The old man's rifled possessions were splayed upon the ground. Tomor sifted through the spoils with a half-searching foot. Enebish watched, picking at a sore on his arm, as the two camels had fat pegs hammered through the soft tissue of their nostrils. One beast was roped to the rear of

Tomor's line. The other, the old man's mount, was led to the back of Enebish's line. It was the job of Bold and The Overseer to burden the two camels with a share of their cargo. At last they got away. As he walked, Enebish held the stone given to him by the old man, keeping it warm in his hand. That night, it started to snow.

The snow fell delicately for two days, a patina of silver-grey ash picking out the knots and rides of the foothills. The high mountains that had been their target for two moons now rose up to meet them. A wail of distant wolves heralded their coming as they trudged on, past boulders and the beckoning archways of cave mouths. Hulks of spent camels blemished the road, bones picked clean, the detritus of caravans past. The Overseer took to walking well ahead of the lines, acting like a forward scout, to make sure the way was clear.

Enebish could see that his master was struggling. The Overseer was hunched low by the weight of responsibility, a load greater than any camel could bear. Only the pipe brought relief. Enebish, by now his unofficial attendant, had become adept at caressing the sludge into a pellet, and holding the bone stem still as the Overseer suckled with loose, sagging lips, gratitude clouding his eyes. After a while, The Overseer, prostrate, would give voice to his soul, half-silently, as Enebish sat cross-legged and monastic, the dutiful novice. Sometimes he would gently move the hair from in front of The Overseer's face. These were the times Enebish cherished. What bound them was theirs alone to share.

The higher the road climbed, the colder it became. The mountain peaks now slipped away behind a veil of white. The snow came down in shaggy tufts, a muffled fleece blanket, comforting only to the eye. Enebish had to brush it roughly from his clothes and hair every few minutes. Panicked by the thought of being lost in a white void, he focused all of his attention on keeping sight of Oktai's train ahead.

The Overseer must have called a stop. There they all were, thick as thieves, under a coal-black overhang of rock. The men were staring at something, hands on hipbones. Enebish entered the huddle and saw a camel. It had been propped up thoughtfully out of the wind, its woollen softness framed against the stratum of cliff behind. The camel's eyes were open, blinking but without expectation, resigned to the irreversible compression of death. It wasn't one of theirs. The Overseer kicked the ground uselessly and cursed. He led them off the road as far as he dared, and they made camp in the deepening snow. The camels bunched together for warmth. In the tent, the men did the same.

The other caravan must be no more than three days ahead, probably less, was The Overseer's assessment. Strike for the pass now and they might run straight into it, especially if the weather was worse higher up. Then again, if they waited, even for a day, to give the other caravan a head-start, they might never get their own camels moving again.

There were two camps in the camp. On one side, The Overseer and Oktai. Hunker down, they counselled, wait for clear skies. Let the other caravan move off. Caution and vigilance had taken them this far. Just a little further. The snow will keep the camels warm, trust in that. On the other side, Bold and Tomor. Why risk everything they have worked for, with the endgame so close? They must jump clear of the beast now before the jaws snap shut. Besides, what did they have to fear, men like them? Once over the pass, they could lose the other caravan and make the final run down to the rendezvous.

In low voices, their conference wore on into the night. To Enebish, the enormity of it all was thrilling. These were the most grown-up of problems. He listened, rapt, with the clear conscience of the runt. Now he understood. All those kicks he'd taken. The taunts. The barbed jibes. The hard knocks. Each of those was a gift, a concession. It meant that, when the time came, nobody would turn to him. Even with their denouement so desperately close, he was free to stay passive, to march or not to march as ordered, to put his destiny in the hands of wiser men.

All was silence. An impasse in the great debate. They lay there, listening to the creak of the tent in the wind. The arrhythmia of tension and release. Finally, The Overseer spoke. Might as well ask the skinny cunt. Gallows laughter. Fading to more silence. So, it's come to this. Four pairs of wolf eyes on Enebish. The fawn. This was real. Enebish didn't cringe. He didn't shy away, because the answer was unequivocal. To side with The Overseer, after everything, surely. Defer to the one who was father to them all, and to Enebish most of all. And yet, there was one overriding truth he had come to know, concerning the lot of the puller and the pulled, the camel and the carcass, the strong and the weak, and it could be distilled into two choices. Walk or die. He chose walk. Bold howled in triumph. The Overseer clicked his tongue. Then it's done. We go with the runt. He lay back, satisfied, and sent Enebish for his pipe.

At dawn they made for the pass. Two camels refused to rise and had to be abandoned. Three more were thrown away before noon, with no attempt made to salvage the cargo. This was grit. Manhandling camels through heavy drift, desperate shouts snatched out of mouths by the swirling blizzard. Pulling, kicking, cursing, falling. This was heroism unsung. Bold, with inhuman resilience, leading the charge, Enebish now his number two, fighting beyond youthful exhaustion. They were a unit, a warband, brothers, pioneers, the great migration. Death matched them step for step as more camels surrendered the fight. And still they pressed on.

By the time they reached the great ovoo marking the apex of the pass, Enebish had no reverence left to give. The rough obelisk of stones was wrapped in blue cloth, an homage to a sky that now lapsed into perilous twilight. They passed it, four trains, depleted, deadened, without circling, without due ceremony. Then over the lip of the crag, the mountain's parting sneer, down to where the wind was quelled. Before them, through the falling snow, waiting, was the rival caravan. The encampment looked half-sunk, quiet as a burial. Surrounding it were camel mounds of drifted snow, a mountain range in miniature, a siege army, petrified as if by some Medusa. Nothing stirred. No demented camp dogs. No tinkle of bells in the wind. All was still.

The Overseer called a stop. Up went the tent. Enebish shrank back as the men readied weapons. Limbs chattering from exhaustion and anticipation. They waited. No sounds but the rumble of their bellies. They waited. Eyelids drooping. Adrenaline flatlining. Nobody came. There was, said The Overseer, no obligation to make contact, according to the customs of camel men. Better the devil you know, muttered Tomor. Perhaps, said Bold, even yet, there were spoils to be gained. Fresh camels. Food and wine for their bellies. A new impasse. Once more, all eyes turned to Enebish. The pawn. Go and see what you can see. Sneak. Stay low. Count the camels. The men if you can. Come back. This is your story now.

Enebish willed himself out of the tent and back into the night. He scurried from rock to rock as the snow whorled and eddied. From exhaustion to delirium now. His legs aflame with effort, he plunged uphill, away from both the camps. Back over the lip, where a great whoosh of air threatened to carry him off into nothingness. And finally, there it was. The ovoo. It was fabulous, metres high, a sculpted megalith of stones, scapula and horse skulls. He reached into his coat to retrieve the old man's stone, and placed it in a niche with so many others.

A pair of eyes watched him intently. It was the lantern glow of both camps, down in the distance. The only lights in a world of darkness. Enebish stood and let himself be drawn towards them. Perspectives wavered. Whether moving uphill or down, now, he couldn't tell. At last he came to a tent. There were camels. Steppe men. He moved forward, and in a soft voice, though not high nor reedy, Enebish announced himself at the threshold.

The snow thickened. Inside the tent, The Overseer was impatient, twitchy. How many? Well? Give him space, fetch tea. They roughed his thin shoulders, expectant. Enebish answered. They are slipping away, he told them. Loading their camels. Expect them to be long gone by morning. The Overseer caught him gently as he fell. The men downed arms. They fished out all the private treats they'd squirrelled away. Wine. liquor. Dice. Pony flesh. This was a celebration. Tomorrow they would make the final run to the rendezvous, a clean break down from the pass. One more sleep, one more run. Then five would become four. Enebish collapsed at the threshold, wasted, the cold harrying his back, Bold flexing his fingers.

That night, the men from the other caravan came. There were six of them, all steppe men. Men of ambition. They worked quickly. Bold was the only one to put up a real fight. For him they used a gun, and finished him with a knife in the throat. He took one of theirs. At the light of dawn, they set to work on the camels and cargo, selecting the strongest animals and taking as much dope as they could add to their own cache.

The tent was pulled down and disposed of. Emptiness reclaimed its space, a blank page. The only traces of struggle, of story, were marks, molasses-black, where the bodies had been dragged away to the rocks. There they were, heaped up in death's embrace, a sprinkling of snow lending unexpected dignity. The Overseer, bloated and blue, still clutched his opium pipe in rictus grip. The pipe that had played his song and betrayed his truths. It had been long and mournful, The Overseer's song. Indulgently unabridged, a deathbed ballad, a murmured chorus of boasts and regrets and confessions, night after night. Enebish had listened carefully, every word, grateful for wisdom.

There were five pullers now, and an overseer. Enebish stood ready at the rearmost train, rope over his shoulder, belly warm, face a mask of concentration. Enebish. Given up by his father to the traders. Determined not to come up short on his first run. Desperate to find the light. To defy the demons. Enebish. Not this one. With a shout, the caravan shunted away in convoy, inching carefully down the loose gravel slope.

FELICITY PEPPER

Focaccia

A brief tale of infatuation in the modern age

Thirteenth of November, 2021.
Her: What are your top three breads? Answers will be scored.
Him: Beigel, sourdough, focaccia.
Her: 1) Beigel – I'm impressed that you've gone for the classic version rather than the standard bagel, this shows great character and an appreciation for the classics in life. Beigel's are a great vehicle for a variety of other delicious foods, which earns you points. 9/10. 2) Sourdough – the one, the only, the bread everyone wanted to shag during lockdown. Popular for a reason, and a connoisseur of avocado. Hip, but a good solid bread with a happy exterior crust. 12/10 because I'm a basic bitch and nothing makes me happier. 3) Focaccia – the divine bread of all breads, the herby mistress herself. An icon, thereby earning extra points (also, I can't count) 18/10.
Him: Okay just want to make it crystal clear that bread review blew me away and am now infatuated.

Fourteenth of November, 2021.
Her: When/how can I ruin your life?
Him: I have a few ideas.

They settle to meet Tuesday daytime. He suggests the Tate Modern because she like art, and she pauses because she doesn't want her favourite place tainted if it's a bad date, but then she agrees. Let's go to the Tate Modern, but you can't be mean to me there because it's my happy place. Can I be mean to your everywhere else? Yes. I like you, he says. He's going to make her focaccia, he swears.

She tells her best friend, who has banned her from dating any more self-proclaimed "artistic types". They just cause you pain, she says, it's a destructive pattern. He's a poet, she tells her best friend. He's funny. Her best friend tells her she's not discussing this anymore if she won't listen to sense: We're in a fight.

147

Eighteenth of November, 2021.
She can't stop thinking about him. She sends him a message asking if he wants to meet tomorrow night. Hell yes, comes his almost instant reply. Come to Kentish Town. She googles him for the first time and watches a performance of his poetry that was shown on Channel 4 a few years ago. She feels her heart beat faster because both he and the poem are so beautiful. She stops after that because she wants to get to know him as a person rather than as a projection. This is the last sensible and realistic feeling she'll have about him.

Nineteenth of November 2021.
She sits on the tube, her mask hiding the fact that she's nervously chewing her lip and gently mouthing the words to Kacey Musgrave's "Cherry Blossom". She likes that the pandemic has given her the freedom to do this and not look mad. She is mad, but this is something it's best to hide from the general public, because singing women on trains fare about as well as a suspected witch in the seventeenth century. She reads a message from her friend, who says that if the date is shit she can come meet her in Primrose Hill instead. As her stop approaches, she panics, worrying that he might ask what she was listening to on her earphones and that she won't have a cool answer. She scrolls through her Spotify, briefly flicking between Kendrick Lamar and then Joy Crookes until she settles on nothing because she's too nervous to listen to music. At Kentish Town she stands on the escalator, travelling up to the surface, with that old familiar feeling of absolute terror than she only gets when meeting someone she might actually like for the first time in a long time. And then she sees him, wearing a black leather jacket and a black wool hat, looking at his phone. She takes a beat before she makes her way over, and then she does something weird and awkward with her body as if to say hey, here I am, please like me, and her mouth says, Hi. He hugs her.

The walk to the pub is full of small talk, about how yes She's been round here before, her friend lived close so we used to come here quite a bit, about Sally Rooney and how He has one of her books but hasn't read it yet, She's on her second book, she started Conversations With Friends after reading Normal People, but she hasn't seen the TV adaptation yet because she wanted to read the book first. She rambles as they wait politely to cross the road – for too long, probably longer than either of them normally would - and she thinks about telling him that actually she accidentally bought Conversations With Friends first when she meant to buy Normal People, because it had a big Normal People sticker on it, which was confusing but also how silly of her – but she doesn't, because She realises that the thought is best left in her head.

He buys her a drink. Double, he asks? Yes please. Later he tells her he isn't a big drinker and she says that's fine, because it is, and she quietly wishes she hadn't had three double gin and tonics. The only table available has some premature candy canes crumbled on the top, so she suggests they sit on the stools by the window. He lets her have the stool with the backrest. His stool is wobbly. She can't remember what they talk about but he knocks his drink over with his elbow and she laughs, but in a kind way. He apologises, but only some of it went on her leg, he got the brunt of it. Well, they'll never dry, they'll be wet forever now. He doesn't immediately pick the glass up, instead choosing to style it out. She finds this charming. He gets himself another drink and then things go a little fuzzy as they get to know each other better. Parents, siblings. His hand is on her leg and she doesn't mind at all. Relationships, sex. He's gently caressing her leg and she finds herself stuck for words, her body blossoming into fire. He stops mid-sentence, smiles, and as if any willpower has left his body, leans into kiss her. She feels the kiss in her deepest crevices and kisses him back. She bites his lip and doesn't mind when he pulls at her hair.

After two drinks, he suggests another pub. As they leave he takes her hand and it is strong and somehow kind but then halfway down the almost empty side street he pushes her up against a wall and kisses her again and she is intoxicated by the way he manages to be both tender and forceful at the same time. He pulls away and says he wants to be alone with her. She shakes her head, she'll be going home, but even now she knows this is a lie. They turn back; he thinks they should go to a different pub than the one he had in mind. But then he stops and pulls her aside again. This time his hands rove her body more freely and when his hand reaches for her throat she catches her breath, a primal feeling taking over. He wants to make her come, he says. She accidentally knocks his hat to a jaunty angle but pulls it back with a sense of politeness. As they begin walking again she realises an earring is missing. He rushes ahead of her to retrace their steps, returning to the scene of each of their crimes. The earring remains elusive and he feels bad because he must have knocked it off in the throes of passion – it was her grandmothers, her mum only gave them to her today, but it's fine, she insists, honestly, it's okay. And she isn't lying, she barely cares about material or sentimental possessions in that moment. He takes her hand again.

There's a small dog in the second, brightly lit pub. They sit on a large leather sofa and he leans back, watching her, as she strokes his leg and they talk about therapy. His started with grief counselling, hers with PTSD. Neither of them asks deeper questions about the reasons, this is an unspoken rule amongst those who go to therapy. He moves closer, and slips his fingers between her legs, surprised to find that she's already wet through her tights. He whispers something in her ear. She whispers back that he can do anything he likes to her, and he replies like what? And she's suddenly shy, unable to articulate herself. But her willpower has dissolved, and she knows she is going home with him, even though she desperately wants to see this man again, even though she knows that sleeping with him might stop that from happening, if the behaviour of other men she's known is any indication. She internally speculates that her lack of self-control will one day be the death of her.

As they leave, she hesitates, because she isn't sure if he's noticed her hand. She never knows the ethical standpoint here, and maybe if she brings it up, it will kill the mood, even if he has noticed it. She only has a vague photo of it on her profile because who likes photos of themselves that show their greatest flaws? She decides he can't have not noticed and swallows her words instead, taking the risk that he'll reject her despite their obvious chemistry. She points out the Franco Manca where she and her friends have had endless nights of wine and pizza – it's so reasonably priced, she quips, which is something that amuses her friends for some reason. He holds her good hand as they walk through Kentish Town, up past the pretty pastel cottages and the Pineapple pub. It's familiar because she knows the area but she also hasn't ever felt so safe with someone she's just met. It's probably the gin. When they get to his flat she drops a pin to her best friend, just to be safe, even though her best friend lives in America and could do fucking nothing if something happened to her. She comments on the big wooden entry door – it's nice. She knows she sounds stupid, just small talk really although she means it, it is a lovely door, but she doesn't think he's judging her.

His dog greets them and she crouches down to stroke him. His coat is silky soft and he grins at her as if he's known her his entire life. I am exactly like a dog, she thinks, falling in love at the drop of a hat and smiling at every possible demon to come my way. Maybe that's why she gets on with dogs so well, loves them so much. Her naivety might be soaked with cynicism but it's still naivety, nonetheless. Although who was it who said that thing about the sentimental person having a hope that things will last, but the romantic soul having a desperate belief that they won't? She remembers later that it was Fitzgerald.

He asks her if she wants anything – water, please. She picks up some books in his bedroom and flicks through them. He has the same desk as her, and she tells him when he returns, passing her a glass of water. Somebody was giving it away, he says. She points at a drawing of a superhero – what's this. Oh, He says, I did that. I help run some workshops and I get involved – I liked that one so I kept it. She feels the blossoms radiate through her body again. He lights a candle and puts Tinashe on his Macbook. He has dried flowers in a vase above his bed and pictures on the walls and she thinks, I could spend time here. It's peaceful.

Then they are on the bed and she feels him envelop her like she's a flower and he's a desperate bee, buzzing into her neck and pulling at her clothes. The dog jumps on to the bed and She laughs. He pushes the dog back down, but kindly, and with a renewed force, pulls down her tights so he can finally feel her for the first time. She doesn't think about condoms even though she should, but how can she when he's touching her like that? This is the stuff you don't learn in sex education or biology or anywhere but the present, when you want someone so badly that you don't care about the consequences. He goes inside her and she is so wet she wonders if he can feel anything at all. He wraps one hand around her neck and they stare into each other's eyes as he rides her. Maybe he's looking without seeing her but she's seeing him, and she reaches back to grab the headboard. He turns her over, eating her out from behind somehow in just the way she likes, before drawing himself back inside her. He spanks her and she wants him to do it again.

He loses his erection, and she knows it's probably the alcohol, or just basic uncooperative, unreliable biology, but later, when he doesn't reply to her texts, she'll wonder if it was because of her, if it was the way she looked, or if it was something she did, because this is the second man that this has happened with. She wants to take him inside her mouth to help, but it's been a long time since she's done that and she's not sure if that's what he wants.

Let's take a break, he says, and he draws her in with one arm. She stills has her bra on – she'd been too caught up in the moment to take it off, flat on her back as she was, but he hadn't seemed to mind, pulling it down and kissing her. Anyway, she reasons, tits generally look great when they're half out of a bra. But now they are both naked apart from her bra and she can't take it off because she's comfortable lying in his arms but also because taking it off at this point might be weirder than leaving it on. They lie for a long time, the music still playing, with flutterings of light conversation. She presses her fingers to his full red lips, tell him they're beautiful. He smiles, his eyes closed. She twirls her fingers around on him absentmindedly and he says he loves it, he loves her hands. She wonders again if he has noticed, if she can make a dark joke as she normally would. He asks her to stay the night. She wants to, but she knows she has to go home and she says so – he cuts her off, it's okay, you don't need a reason, almost like he's embarrassed to have even asked. She falls silent and then explains: my son has rugby in the morning and he forgot his boots and his key, so I have to get back. It brings the pedestrian into the magic in the bedroom and she worries she's ruined something, but then it passes. Her train isn't for an hour, so they settle in for a cuddle, falling asleep and missing it entirely. I'll get the next one. We should probably leave now, he says, to be sure. They get dressed, he puts the dog on the lead, and they step out into the cold November air, holding hands. She's glad she brought her coat and she says so. It's faux fur, the same colour as the night sky.

At the train station, he asks if she wants him to wait with her – she does, the train isn't for another 20 minutes, but she says no, because he looks so tired. He kisses her again, long and deep. Let me know when you're on the train, he says. Let me know when you're home. I will. He talks about seeing her on Tuesday and bringing her focaccia – she says, oh yes, where was my focaccia today? He seems put out and says he never promised focaccia for today. I know, I know, I'm only joking, she says. He kisses her again and this time she feels like light, because she knows she'll see him again. Later, she'll look back at that moment and cry. Silly little fool.

On the platform a young man approaches her. He's a student, he says, he's studying business. He's from San Paulo. Where was she tonight? A date. Him too. He asks to sit next to her on the train and because she's in such a good mood she lets him. He tries very hard to flirt with her but her mind is elsewhere, still back in His bedroom, still kissing his neck and brushing up again his soft, warm skin. San Paulo shows her photos of his dogs back in Brazil. When he gets off the train, the man sitting in front of her turns around. He's probably in his early twenties. That was the most platonic conversation I've ever heard in my life, he says, was that a date? No, he wasn't my date. It must have been a good date that you went on? Yes. He asks what she does and she tells him what she tells everyone – she's between jobs – she left her old one and is waiting for a new job to start in December. This is true but it's not completely true. She's been off sick from her current job since September, after having a mental breakdown and being unable to cope with the pressure.

He asks her what she's going to do with her time off, and when she says she's going to write, and walk the dog, he laughs patronisingly. Why don't you go travelling or something? He says. Because I have a 12 year old child. He doesn't believe her. But you're what, like, 21? She laughs. How much have you had to drink. I'm 33. She remembers that earlier in the night He had said he liked that they were the same age – it was a throwaway comment but maybe he usually dates younger women? Anyway, she says to the man on the train, how old are you? You have to guess. She pulls a face. Twelve, she says. He asks what social media she uses. Instagram and Twitter. He laughs. Twitter's for boomers. What's your Instagram handle? It's on private, she says, you won't see anything. He insists. It is her name. He mocks her low number of followers and she is bemused that he thinks followers make a difference, that he thinks she might care about how many people like the photos she puts on a private account. They're just snapshots of memories, that's all. She realises that things never change, people in their early twenties will always hinge everything on being popular. When she gets home she'll see that the second young man has requested to follow her. She'll laugh gently and reject the request. When he leaves the train she takes a smiling selfie and sends it to Him: Just got told I look 21 – thanks for the youth giving sex! It was an honour and a pleasure, he'll reply.

Twentieth of November, 2021
She wakes up feeling terrible and is a little bit sick – apparently alcohol and vigorous sex paired with little sleep doesn't agree with her – but she is on a cloud of happiness. He wants to see me again, she texts her best friend. I think he made me squirt for the first time in my life. What did it feel like? It felt good, I didn't orgasm, but it's hard to describe – I just felt good. Is that normal? I looked on the internet and apparently it is. It's never happened before, to either of them. They're fascinated. She orders McDonalds and send her best friend another message. I'm not being funny but he's adorable and I must have him.

He isn't responsive that day, but she reasons with herself that he's probably tired. He asks her how her day's been and she tell him she ordered Mcdonalds. I love McDonald's breakfast, he says. The eggs worry me, she replies. He replies with a voicenote that begins very seriously, saying he doesn't want to be rude but he must be honest with her, making her heart drop – is he about to tell her that he's not interested? – before saying that she can't tell him she worries about the eggs because then he'll worry about the eggs. He's on his way to get a KFC. She responds telling him the eggs are obviously very normal, regular eggs, and then mentions that there's a brothel above the KFC in her town and the rumour always was that the mayonnaise was tainted. He tells her he isn't going to listen to the rest of the message, but the rest of the message was her telling him he's sweet for walking her to the train station, apologising if he's tired and telling him about the boys on the train. She sends a faux letter apologising for her fast food slander. He sends her a selfie of him and his dog and she responds with three heart eye emojis. Then she sends him a video of her apologising again: I don't want to ruin fast food for you, I only want to ruin you. He doesn't respond. She doesn't hear from him on Sunday. She regrets sending the video.

She romanticises everything, becoming infatuated rarely, but easily. There has been a short string of unrequited and intense loves throughout her life. When she was eight she fell in love for the first time, with a blue eyed blonde boy a few years above. He was sweet and very tolerant of her declarations of love, which she wrote in little letters for him to dutifully read. He even allowed her to kiss him once, on the ear. Quite why she chose the ear she's not sure, but then she's never really chosen the most common path. One day, she pushed her luck too far, boldly delivering him his weekly love letter in front of his friends, who promptly mocked them both. The kind boy went red to the very ears that she adored so much, and tore the letter up, scattering the pieces in the school's wildlife garden. She ran away and cried in the toilets and was berated by a teacher when she said her heart was broken. Don't be foolish, the teacher scoffed, you're eight years old, you don't know what love is. But She did, and the feeling has been the same ever since. That sickness when someone doesn't return her love, like something is tearing inside of her. The feeling never changes, it's just the faces and her supposed level of maturity that alter at all.

On Monday evening he sends her a voicenote. He's sorry for the radio silence, he's been busy, or no he hasn't, he doesn't know why he didn't message. He's excited to see her tomorrow, he says, but by the way he has a gig in the evening so he'll have to leave before then. She listens to the voicenote while she walks her dog down the embankment lit with pretty lights, and she can't stop smiling. He's excited to see her. He's going to make her focaccia. Her mind goes where it usually does with these things – over the top and to a ridiculous place of hope. She imagines seeing him, him scooping her into his arms and kissing her again. She wonders if he'll kiss her right away; if he'll present the focaccia as someone would present a bouquet flowers to make her laugh. She doesn't realise she's projecting her own fantasies of what he isn't onto him. Her imagination has been starved for so long, she's been so blocked and unable to write down her own stories. Depression can act like a plug and there's nowhere for the thoughts to go but around and around. She doesn't recognise this until later, when there's no longer any hope and the dream is extinguished. But when she does, she can write again. And so in that way, she was right, he was special, because he helped her break down that wall without even knowing it.

On Tuesday morning he sends her a voicenote and she knows what it says before she even opens it. He didn't respond last night when she asked what time they'd be meeting. She avoids listening and when she does, her heart sinks. He has to cancel because he needs to work, but he's so apologetic. He wants to reschedule for Friday. It seems genuine, she thinks. But she can feel the dream, the fancy bird cage she's trapped her ideal of them in, collapsing around her. She doesn't respond right away. She walks the dog around the park twice, thinking she'll voicenote him then, but she doesn't, she just enjoys the sun instead, and her dog dancing along beside her, and the crunching orange leaves of autumn underfoot. She has a shower when she gets home and lays on her bed in a white towel. She understands, she tells him, if he has to work he has to work. And she means what she's saying but inside the familiar doubt rises as she hears the voice of her mother, of society, telling her that sleeping with men on the first date causes them to lose interest. She doesn't truly believe this – some of the best relationships she knows started with a first date fuck – but it's an idea that haunts her. What if this is her fault, her lack of self-control and discipline will lead her to spend the rest of her life alone, just to be used periodically by men.

She avoids messaging him the next two days because she doesn't want to disturb him if he's working. She sends a voicenote on Wednesday evening. It's simple and she gives it a lot of thought before she sends it, because she tends to ramble on voicenotes ever since she discovered that you didn't need to hold the record button down the entire time. Her friends are tolerant of these increasingly inane ramblings, and usually respond back in kind, supporting her in whatever mad thing she's banging on about, but she doesn't want to expose this side of her, particularly if he's losing interest. It doesn't really occur to her yet that her comfort has shifted because she knows, deep down, that this is it, this is all she'll ever have from him. One night, and a few promises of focaccia with benefits.

He doesn't reply.

She deliberates over his silence. She isn't working so she has the time to stew in her own thoughts. She had asked him to meet on Saturday rather than Friday, but he didn't respond. She browses his Instagram – his videos make her laugh, and she feels a pang each time. On Thursday afternoon she sends him a text. I hope I'm wrong but I feel like maybe you're blowing me off? I'd rather know if that's the case. I have a delicate little heart, you can't be toying with it with promises of focaccia (joking). He comes online but the double ticks remain grey. By the evening she can feel her heart, torn and ragged from too much rejection, reluctantly continuing to pump blood around her body that's probably, according to society, past its sell by date. She feels the anger, the shallow bed of regret. Why didn't you settle for one of those nice boring boys? You could be trapped in Bedford forever in a dull and lifeless marriage with a man who votes Lib Dem, but at least you wouldn't be alone, at least you wouldn't be going through this torment. She has a glass of wine and a back and forth with her best friend. We should start a game where we compile all the red flags of every man you've dated and then guess which one belongs to who, her best friend jokes. Maybe I should do report cards, She jokes. After all, I start off with bread reviews, why not end the infatuation with a review of the man if he's ghosting me. It'll probably be cathartic.

She pours another glass of wine, opens her Macbook and starts a new document. Report Card, she writes.

Twenty-sixth of November, 2021
She wakes up early and checks to see if He has replied. Two grey ticks, still. She goes and makes herself a cup of tea, takes her Citalopram, and lets the dog outside, arbitrary motions that keep her alive. She opens Whatsapp again. She sends the report card. Then she deletes his number, clears the chat, and unmatches him on Bumble. Alexa, play Phoebe Bridgers. She never expected to get focaccia, not really.

HILARY TAYLOR

Some creatures trapped in ice

The moose

was trapped in a frozen river in Sweden. Firefighters set her free with ice axes and ropes, warmed her with blankets and a massage, hacked a path to dry land and coaxed her through it, tied a blue ribbon round her neck and let her go. Or an ice skater found her when it was too late and posted a photograph on Instagram.

The polar bear

was a plastic one, no bigger than my thumb, submerged in a pot of water and placed in the freezer overnight. Five-year-old you chipped at the ice with a toy hammer until the animal was free. She emerged as she went in – hard, unfeeling, cold.

The nematode worm

slept in Siberian permafrost for forty thousand years. Hardy and resourceful, she had a knack for protecting herself. The permafrost wasn't perma after all. When it thawed, the worm came to life, undamaged. She moved and ate. Clear signs.

You

were damaged before the ice wrapped its cold fingers around you, squeezed you in its iron grip. I watch you through the bluish tinge but you refuse to meet my gaze. Suspended, numb and dumb, you wait, flesh as stone. When I approach with my ice axe, my hammer, my blankets and ropes and my blue ribbon, I fear it is too late. Your skin is scarred from previous attempts to release you from your frozen shield, your sanctuary. I down tools, and wait for a slow, natural thaw. I long for clear signs.

JELLE CAUWENBERGHS

Yesterday, They Crossed the Elbe

One of them stands sleeveless by the oxbow in the wolf-grey dawn, giving directions, while his friend steers a heavy boat towards me. Trying to catch me. Bitterns watch from the reeds. I float by, chewing on a dragonfly. The boy in the boat shouts. He has spotted more "logs." Further upstream, there is a meadow where men lie at odd angles in the wet grass, jewelled in cobwebs. They glow at night, bright as moonstones. Women from the village have stuffed their mouths with straw so the ants will not make nests inside them and take their souls. Their hair is frozen white, sheathed in ice after the late frost. The boys dread these thawing corpses. They fear the rustle of skin in the dark. Waking the adders. Hissing in their disturbed winter sleep. *Mercy. Mistake. Mother.* Mothers they have not seen in a hundred years. Mothers in another language. Are they the same mothers? These soft, muted bassoons? A few days earlier, the boys rolled a few of us into the river. They feel guilty now. The boys argue. Nothing can be done. Our bodies are heavy. I hear silences within silences. Then the slippery babble of the boat as it disappears around the bend, the paddle slicing the water, leaving no trace. The boys have gone home. The booming cry of the bitterns suddenly rings from the reeds, and the resurgence of my hope for salvation surprises me, as slow clouds rise in the East.

GOLDIE GOLDBLOOM

In the Museums of Heaven and Hell

On either side of the halls of Heaven and Hell are the great glass-fronted cases displaying the glories of this world. Heaven has the stonefish, the blue-ringed octopus, all five-thousand varieties of coral polyp, the smallest tooth of the sperm whale, the trembling light from a star that died millions of years earlier, the last time a baby nurses from its mother, the look in the eyes of old friends when they meet after a long absence. Hell has scalped tickets to a Rolling Stones concert, a bathroom scale, a plagiarized essay with an A in red ink at the top, a speedometer, a whiff of perfume, the words a CEO used about the least of his employees, shame, humiliation, disgrace, a tiny white flag.

Still waiting to be catalogued appropriately: the roar of the wind down the valley at night when you are feeling lonely; the coin you dropped unwillingly in the hand of the addict begging outside the 7-11; the ragged, badly-fitting wig and the fifty extra pounds you wear in order to appear less attractive to men who might hurt you; the memory of your ex-husband's face like a desiccated bone stripped of its meat; the soft fur of moss that grows on the side of your children that didn't receive enough sunshine; the irrational love you carry for people who do not love you back.

BARBARA DIGGS

That Time You Went to Space

When the bomb rolled out of Rennie's mouth and smashed down onto the dinner table, there was just time enough for you to marvel at how something as tiny and weightless as a single word could land with such impact, but then the shockwave blasted you into the exosphere, where you hung by ice-numbed fingertips on the dark curve of space, gaping at the devastated table below; the splintered wine glasses, the slap of burgundy on white linen, crystal shards winking from the spinach salad, and the gravy-spattered guests, who avoided looking at where you were or where you had been because Ellen had put so much effort into the Chicken Marsala and Rennie didn't mean it like *that*, of course, and because as long as they didn't look toward your chair or see you fighting to breathe at the edge of space, dinner would not be ruined, nothing would have happened, so they continued to eat with their heat-twisted silverware, picking at mushrooms from between the cracks in their plates, crooning in such soothing, honey-sweet tones that you found yourself descending back to the table, eating alongside them, wondering whether there really had been a bomb and whether you really had gone to space, and you were almost convinced that you'd imagined it all except that with every bite, glass crunched between your teeth and your tongue was absolutely lacerated.

HELEN IRVING

Valentine's Day

My radio alarm clock blinking in waltz time. A heart-shaped stain arranged on my bedsheet. The imprint of a hand, naked on the shower screen. My shoes, toes together as if they were talking. A squirrel begging while my cat eats its breakfast. A cobweb, like a dream-catcher, frozen on the door knob. A hole in the sky claiming to be the moon. Footprints at my gate stencilled in ice. My neighbour's husband putting luggage in his car. Brown moss with white frosting on a terracotta pot. Tiny shoots of spring bulbs like clitorises in the soil. A flyer in my driveway, offering holidays in Iceland. A slug trail mimicking a ladder in my stocking. The roots of a tree raised up like dancers' ankles. Claw prints of sparrows like dancing lesson steps. Dirty words written by the sun on my windscreen. A boy delivering roses in a plastic laundry basket. Men in dark suits holding red balloons. A woman with two dogs cradled in a blanket. Throbbing red lights on a passing police car. Oil-slicked water coloured with confetti. Two schoolgirls, heads together, sharing a soft drink. A couple holding hands, going the wrong way. Cracks in the pavement like a Jackson Pollock painting. Cloud shapes overhead trying to look winsome. A child in a jacket embroidered with violets. Empty champagne bottles sitting on a brick wall. Rose petals in the carpark leading to nowhere. My neighbour's number crying on my mobile.

KATIE PIPER

Autopsy of a Mother

On her headstone it says, *In Memory of a Loving Mother,* and she died right here, on this blotched concrete, next to these plastic chairs.

The ice-cream van swirled its red and white lolly siren thick and loud. She lay with two ice-creams in each hand, oozing towards her ears and her hair. Her thumb crushed into a cone.

There was a silver bracelet on her left wrist, trinkets of unicorns, keys and stars patterned across her empty vessels – the cold metal ringing.

She wore a cream dress dappled with lily stamens and grey eucalypt leaves. The elastic sides had relented for a belly of four pillows, one for each child.

She had a mermaid tattoo, scales inked around fine metatarsals.

They say they found layers, the first was the thickest – rubbery, impermeable. A layer of tolerance.

The next layer was thinner, semipermeable.

When they held it up to the light there were clocks ticking, all telling different times.

There were poems, leaves rustling.

There were kisses, and Eastern Spoonbills – plucking, trilling, tucking.

Beneath her left breast was the shoe of her grandfather, still with the wad he'd used to cover a hole.

The last layer was a glimmer,

a soft sea of words sewn,

and all ears listening to her, and lawns of space for her, and money spools unfurling for her – a safe house.

And then her pelvic ring, they said, was a bucket for her sacred –

red sequins,

purple sequins,

feathers.

The dancer no one knew.

HANNAH RETALLICK

Falling Woman

willingly, on the strange-office-party canal boat between Shrewsbury and Somewhere, where you told me I was worth more than I knew

dancing at New Year's, feeling on my hip how much you wanted to begin it with me, despite her

in the *Othello* interval, squeezed with wine-sipping foyer crowds, seeing you hand your last unsoiled Kleenex to a sneezing woman, even though you would sniff through the final act

when I told you the shocking news and you promised we could sort it out together

squeezed into a McDonald's booth afterwards, staring at cold ketchupped fries and feeling your hand comfort mine, pressing it into the sticky table

during our first summer, as I marked your lips with Rimmel's Asia and gratitude because you told me you had finally got around to it

opening the box, realising the yellow diamond wasn't fake

seeing the shaking tux at the end of the lily-lined aisle

following years of trying, listening to you reassure me it was still the right decision all that time ago and we were happy enough without, weren't we?

as you explained what I saw, and that it was my fault really, but you still loved me despite my flaws and it wouldn't happen again

when you dabbed my sliced face with a soaked pad of antiseptic and remorse

and even now, as you pretend to disintegrate on the kitchen floor and beg me to change my mind

I fall.

DAVID SWANN

The Life of Fibonacci, Shaped to Resemble a Galaxy or Pine Cone

Loafer.
Traveller.
AKA Simpleton.
Famous as Fibonacci.
Who brought the zero north.
And was preoccupied by the sex-lives of rabbits.
Then rhymed their breeding with the sequence of swirls in a goat's horn.
And taught his fellow Pisans to understand the beauty of their temples, built on patterns discovered by those architects, the trees.
Fibonacci, I thought of you today when my mathematics colleague with the lovely nose – set in that golden perch between eyes and chin – said I'd never know reality until I learned to speak maths.
If they called you simpleton, it must have been from the confusion Einstein later warned us to avoid – to make things as simple as possible, but never *more* simple – a teaching I remembered while measuring the precise ratio of my colleague's face, wishing I was some ancient sage, capable of finding worlds inside my zeroes.
Dreaming as I gazed, and sad I'd never speak maths, I saw you trekking through Algeria's deserts with numbers in your saddlebag – the numbers that are pretty much all that remains of you now.
Loafer, voyager, simpleton – you taught us a lesson we're all forever learning: that everything counts down to the same old nothing.
So time has followed its pre-determined sequence and erased your life's last traces.
Hence, we find you now in strange places.
Galaxies' tails, eyes of hurricanes.
A nautilus's shell.
Iris petals.
Noses.
This.

(232 words, Fibonacci sequence 1, 1, 2, 3, 5, 8, 13, 21, 34, 55 – then backwards from 34).

Biographies

Inua Ellams was born in Nigeria and is a touring poet, playwright and performer. He is an ambassador for the Ministry of Stories and his books of poetry include *Candy Coated Unicorns* and *The Half-God of Rainfall* – an epic story in verse. He recently completed his first full poetry collection *The Actual*. He lives and works from London, where he founded the Midnight Run, a nocturnal urban excursion. Inua is a Fellow of the Royal Society of Literature.

Kathy Fish has published five collections of short fiction including *Wild Life: Collected Works 2003-2018*. Her work has appeared in *Ploughshares*, *Copper Nickel*, *Washington Square Review*, and numerous other journals, textbooks and anthologies. Kathy's *Collective Nouns for Humans in the Wild* was selected for Best American Nonrequired Reading 2018 and the current edition of *The Norton Reader*. She is the recipient of a Ragdale Foundation Fellowship and a Copper Nickel Editors' Prize.

Tim Pears left school at sixteen and had many jobs including trainee welder, assistant librarian, fruit picker, nursing assistant and builder. All the time he was writing. He eventually became a short story writer, film maker and novelist.

His collection of short stories *Chemistry and Other Stories* was published in 2021 by Bloomsbury and chosen by the *Sunday Times* for their best new short story collections. They declared it 'as good as any modern fiction you will read this year.'

Tim's novel *In a Land of Plenty* was made into a BBC drama series. He was shortlisted for the Royal Society of Literature Ondaatje Prize, the IMPAC Dublin Literary Award and is a Fellow of the Royal Society of Literature.

In his spare time Tim remains 'an avid spectator of the amazing human invention that is the game of football.'

Writers' Biographies

Nicole Adabunu is an MFA Poetry Candidate at the Iowa Writers' Workshop as an Iowa Arts Fellow. Her work has been published by Writer's Digest, The Academy of American Poets, a 2022 Anthology selected by former Poet Laureate Billy Collins, and elsewhere. She currently lives and writes in Iowa City.

Peter Adamson founded *New Internationalist* magazine in 1970 then became Senior Adviser to UNICEF (1980–1996) with responsibility for its flagship publications including the annual *State of the World's Children report*. He also wrote and presented BBC television's annual documentary '*Global Report*' (1984–1988). From 2000 to 2012 he edited UNICEF's *Report Card* on child poverty in rich nations. He has published three novels – *Facing out to Sea* (Sceptre, 1996), *The Tuscan Master* (Sceptre, 2000) and *The Kennedy Moment* (Myriad Editions, 2018). He has also published a non-fiction book (*Landmark in Time*, 2021).

Chaun Ballard is a poetry faculty member in Alaska Pacific University's Low-Residency MFA Program, a doctoral student of poetry at University of Nebraska-Lincoln, an affiliate editor for Alaska Quarterly Review, an assistant poetry editor for *Terrain.org*, and a graduate of the MFA Program at the University of Alaska Anchorage. Chaun Ballard's chapbook, *Flight*, won the 2018 Sunken Garden Poetry Prize published by Tupelo Press. His poems have appeared in *Narrative Magazine*, *New York Quarterly*, *The New York Times*, *Terrain.org* and *Tupelo Quarterly* amongst others. His work has received nominations for Best New Poets, Best of the Net, and Pushcart Prizes.

Freya Bantiff (previously Carter) was the winner of the Canterbury Poet of the Year competition 2021. A member of Hive Poetry, she was longlisted for the Winchester Poetry Prize in 2022, won second prize in the Bedford Poetry Competition 2021, and was the winner of the Walter Swan Poetry Prize (for 18-25) in 2020, alongside the Timothy Corsellis Poetry Prize in 2017. Freya's poems and stories have been placed in the Aesthetica Creative Writing Award (2021), Mslexia Flash Fiction Competition (2020), the Ilkley Literature Poetry Festival (2010–2015) and Foyle Young Poet of the Year (2015).

Roberta Beary writes to connect with the silenced, to let them know they are heard. Their first poetry collection, *The Unworn Necklace*, was selected as a Poetry Society of America finalist. Their prose poem chapbook, *Deflection*, won a Haiku Society of America book award and was a finalist for the Touchstone and Eric Hoffer awards. Their forthcoming second collection, *Carousel*, won the Snapshot Press book award. Their words appear in *Rattle, The New York Times, Best Microfiction, Best Small Fictions*, and other publications. Born in New York City, they divide their time between the USA and the west of Ireland.

Jelle Cauwenberghs was born in Belgium and studied English Literature in France. He was a runner-up for the Desperate Literature Short Fiction Prize in 2020 and longlisted in 2022. He was shortlisted for The London Magazine Poetry Prize in 2021. He works as a bookseller in Glasgow while pursuing postgraduate research in modern art, poetry, and translation at Sorbonne Nouvelle in Paris.

Abi Curtis is professor of creative writing at York St John University. She is the author of two poetry collections, *Unexpected Weather* and *The Glass Delusion* (Salt) and a novel, *Water & Glass* (Cloud Lodge). She has had stories placed in the Fish Prize and Alpine Fellowship Prize and has been the recipient of an Eric Gregory Award and a Somerset Maugham Award. She regularly collaborates with artists, musicians and scientists and is currently editing a collection of writing on early parenthood for The Emma Press.

Janet Dean was brought up in a mining community in South Yorkshire and now lives in York. Following a forty-year career in the public sector, she was awarded an MA in Creative Writing in 2015, after which she co-founded Awakening The Writer Within, running workshops and retreats. Her poetry has been shortlisted in the Bridport Prize (2012), commended in the Poetry Society's Stanza Poetry Competition and featured in the Northern Poetry Library's 50th anniversary Poem of the North. As Janet Dean Knight she writes fiction; her first novel *The Peacemaker* was published in 2019 and launched at York Literature Festival.

Barbara Diggs is an American writer living in Paris, France. Her fiction has been published in numerous literary journals and appears in the 2021 Bath Flash Fiction Award Anthology. She also writes non-fiction books for middle grade students on topics of race and history. She is currently at work on a historical novella-in-flash.

Jenny Doughty is originally British but has lived in Maine since 2002. She is a former English teacher, and Education Adviser to Penguin Books UK, where she edited an anthology of pre-20th century poetry *Key Poets* and wrote two children's non-fiction books under the name Jenny Green. In the USA, her poems have been featured in *Naugatuck River Review, Four Way Review, Fib Review, Hole in the Head Review,* and *Sin Fronteras* among others, and in various anthologies. Her first collection of poetry, *Sending Bette Davis to the Plumber*, was published by Moon Pie Press in September 2017.

Trent England's fiction has appeared in print and online in *Conjunctions, Hobart, The Masters Review,* and more. He has twice been nominated for the Pushcart Prize and was named a Best Microfiction winner in 2020 for his story "A Quick Word About my Life", which first premiered at *Okay Donkey*. His most recent play, *Solitaire Suite*, had its world premiere in 2021, and he is currently in pre-production for his newest play, *Entanglement*. He lives with his wife and their son and daughter in Duxbury, Massachusetts, a small, seaside town, where he is also a stay-at-home dad.

Johnny Eugster grew up in Hong Kong and studied Mandarin at London University's School of Oriental and African Studies. He then became a copywriter working in London and Hong Kong finally opening his own advertising agency in Shanghai. He now lives with his family in Stroud, Gloucestershire. It is here he achieved a major milestone of owning his own tractor. Hardly a day goes by when his Kubota L2850 is not buffed up and swooned over. When not flirting with tractors, he kite surfs, mountain bikes and writes. He is a postgraduate of the MA Creative Writing at Bath Spa University.

Beatrice Garland is a psychologist who spent her working life in the National Health Service, as clinician, teacher and researcher. She has been a writer for most of her life, publishing both professional texts and poetry. In 2001 she won the National Poetry Competition, and in 2002 the Strokestown International Competition. She has published two books of poetry *The Invention of Fireworks*, and *The Drum,* the first of which was short-listed for the Forward Prize for a first collection and is on the verge of completing a third book of poems about early research in the science of immunology.

Lindsay Gillespie was born in South Wales, and lives in the South Downs. In between she has been a graphic designer and illustrator, lived in Delhi and taught English in Tokyo. She writes short and not-so-short stories and was a Costa 2021 Short Story Award finalist. Story Radio has featured her work on its podcast. She was shortlisted for Oxford Flash Fiction, Fiction Factory and long listed for Exeter Short Story. Her writing has just been published in The Rhys Davies Short Story Award Anthology. She is currently finishing a short story collection about outsiders. Twitter: @LindsGillesp14

Goldie Goldbloom is an internationally published writer of fiction and nonfiction. She is the recipient of fellowships from the National Endowment for the Arts, the City of Chicago, the Brown Foundation and Yaddo. Her most recent novel won the French Bookseller's Prize for Fiction (2021) and the National Jewish Library Award (2020). Previously, her novel, *The Paperbark Shoe*, was placed on the NEA Big Reads list (2018) and won the AWP Novel Award (2011). Her writing has appeared in *Ploughshares*, the *Kenyon Review*, on NPR and in *Le Monde*. She is a single mother of eight and an LGBTQ advocate.

Lara Haworth has been published in magazines including *Visual Verse*, *Biography, LAKE, ACME, Nōd* and *Feels*. Her new film, *All the People I Hurt with My Wedding*, launched on the platform She Does Filmz in April 2021. In October 2021 she was commissioned to write a play, *Drowning in a Sea of Love*, for Tour de Moon 2022. In February 2022, her poem, *The Thames Barrier*, was highly commended by Philip Gross in the Café Writers Poetry Competition. Her debut novel, *The Straits*, is represented by Jo Bell at Bell Lomax Moreton. *Monumenta* is adapted from her second novel.

Malcolm Heyhoe was born and raised in a small town in Lancashire, and now lives in Nottingham with his wife. He was a racing journalist and flagship tipster for the Sporting Life and Racing Post Weekender. His stories have been longlisted for the Short Fiction Journal, Fish, and Bath International Short Story prizes. He is working on a collection of short stories and recently completed a humorous novel, an ensemble piece, with six main characters, moving quickly, with lots of gregarious dialogue.

Helen Irving is a recently retired Australian academic. She lives in Sydney with her husband, but (Covid permitting) spends several months each year in London and elsewhere in the world. She is the author of five non-fiction books and much journalism, but lives a parallel life as a fiction writer, with several unpublished novels and numerous short stories, some of which have been long or shortlisted in competitions. Her only previous award, years ago, was for an ABC five-minute radio story. She does not regard herself otherwise as a miniaturist but is beginning to wonder.

P. Kearney Byrne's stories have appeared in *The Stinging Fly, The White Review, The Dublin Review, Banshee, Per Contra* and other journals in Ireland and the USA. Her awards include the *Penguin Ireland/Sunday Business Post, Francis McManus and John McGahern Award*. She has twice been long-listed in the Sunday Times Audible competition and was shortlisted in the 2021 *White Review* short story prize. Phil has an MA in Creative Writing from UCD and is working on a novel assisted by funding from the Arts Council Ireland. She is represented by Judith Murray of Greene and Heaton Literary Agency, London.

Nairn Kennedy is a Leeds-based poet whose work has appeared in, amongst others, *Orbis, Ink Sweat & Tears, The London Magazine, Stand, The North* and *Under the Radar*. He's been a prize winner in the Ilkley Literature Festival Competition, has been longlisted in the National Poetry Competition, and commended in the Hippocrates Prize, and several others. Other activities he enjoys besides poetry include (occasional) walking in the Yorkshire countryside, gardening and writing computer software. Find him on Twitter @nairnkennedy

Lance Larsen is the author of five poetry collections, most recently *What the Body Knows* (Tampa 2018). His poems have appeared in *TLS, London Magazine, Poetry Magazine, Paris Review, New York Review of Books, New England Review,* and *Best American Poetry 2009*. His awards include a Pushcart Prize and a fellowship from the National Endowment for the Arts. He teaches at Brigham Young University and likes to fool around with aphorisms: "When climbing a new mountain, wear old shoes." In 2017 he completed a five-year appointment as Utah's poet laureate.

Kerry Lyons is a writer, researcher, and PhD candidate at RMIT University, Melbourne. Her story *Contrapuntal Motion* was shortlisted in the Stringybark Short Story Awards in 2022. She lives in Australia and is the mother of three children, guardian of two cats, and sporadic grower of vegetables. In previous iterations of her life, she has been a photographer and a secondary school English teacher. Her writing occurs in the fleeting gaps between work, study and parenting, a situation which has provoked an enduring love of the short story form.

Paul Matthews, author of the creative writing sourcebook, *Sing Me the Creation* (Hawthorn Press), contributes to the 'Storytelling Beyond Words' course at Emerson College in East Sussex where he has been a long-time lecturer and community poet. He travels widely in the UK and elsewhere, giving readings of his poetry and encouraging through playful exercises a love of the written and spoken word. He co-founded the summer school, 'Poetry OtherWise'. Books of his poetry include *Verge* (Arc Publications), *The Ground that Love Seeks* (Five Seasons Press) and *This Naked Light* (Troubadour). He helps teachers bring imaginative language into their classrooms.

Damien Murphy lives in Dublin, Ireland with his wife and daughter. His writing has appeared in *The Irish Independent*, *The Big Issue*, *The Sunday Business Post*, and *The Dublin Inquirer*. He was shortlisted for the RTE Short Story Award. He is currently working on a collection of short stories.

Damen O'Brien is a multi-award-winning Australian poet. His prizes include The Moth Poetry Prize, the Newcastle Poetry Prize, the Peter Porter Poetry Prize, the Welsh International Poetry Competition, the Cafe Writer's Poetry Competition and the Magma Judge's prize. His poems have been published or are forthcoming in many journals including *Meanjin, Cordite, Southerly, Overland, Island, Poetry Wales, New Ohio Review, Mississippi Review, Touchstone* and *New Millennium*. Damen's first book of poetry, *Animals With Human Voices*, was published in 2021 through Recent Work Press. He's on Twitter at @damen_o

Yseult Ogilvie was born in London but lived in New York until she was ten. She studied Architecture at Oxford Brookes University, and post-grad at The Bartlett, University College London. Several of her short stories have been published in anthologies including *The London Magazine*, The Macmillan/Scotland on Sunday Short Story Competition collection, and *The Mammoth Book of New Erotica*. She has written two novels one of which, *Redpoint*, was published online by The Pigeonhole. She is currently working on her third novel. She lives in Somerset.

Thomas O'Malley grew up in southeast England and studied English Literature at university. He has had several writing jobs including working as an editor for Marvel Comics and a guidebook author for Lonely Planet. Thomas lived in Beijing for 12 years, staying in the old part of the city and going on occasional rambles along the Great Wall. He is currently in the UK with his family, working as a copywriter and scriptwriter. He thanks Covid, hesitantly, for giving him the excuse to write a short story.

Felicity Pepper lives in Bedford. She is mother to a teenager (biological) and a Shih Tzu (adopted). She studied English Literature at Goldsmiths as a mature student after dropping out of school at seventeen, and now works as an Executive Assistant at a PR agency. In a past life she wrote gig reviews for *Artrocker*. She has always written stories (and some very bad angst-ridden poetry as a teenager) but has rarely shared her work. She has only entered one writing competition before; she won a book about storms, and it was very exciting (she was six). Instagram / Twitter: @probablyflick

Katie Piper was raised in the UK. She left for the Middle East in her early twenties, and now resides in Northeast Victoria, Australia. Katie is a nurse and a mother. She began to write during maternity leave, first in a tweet size story challenge on Twitter. Her work has since been anthologised by Reflex Press, National Flash Fiction Day, and Rare Swan Press. Katie has also been published by Ellipsis Zine, X-ray literary Mag and The Cabinet of Head. In 2020 Katie was a Pushcart nominee, and in 2021 she was longlisted for the Commonwealth Short Story Prize.

Hannah Retallick is from Anglesey, North Wales. She was home educated and then studied with the Open University, graduating with a first-class BA (Honours) Arts and Humanities (Creative Writing and Music) degree, before passing her Creative Writing MA with distinction. In 2018, Hannah started to send out her short stories on a regular basis. Since then, she has been published in paperbacks, in e-books, and online, as well as placed/shortlisted in several international competitions. She is currently working on a flash fiction collection, a short story collection, a novella, and a novel. https://www.hannahretallick.co.uk/about

Kate Rutter has been an actor in Film, TV, Theatre and Radio for many years. She has been lucky enough to work with directors such as Mike Leigh and Ken Loach, whose film *I, Daniel Blake* won the Palme d'Or. Kate is an MA Writing graduate of Sheffield Hallam University. Her poems have been published widely in anthologies and journals such as *The Rialto*, *The North* and *Magma* and she was Highly Commended in the

2021 Poetry Business International Pamphlet Competition. She has been longlisted, shortlisted and this year Highly Commended for The Bridport Prize. Cold water swimming is her only vice.

David Swann has now had eleven successes at the Bridport Prize, whose flash fiction contest he judged in 2013. Last year, his book, *Season of Bright Sorrow* (Ad Hoc Press), won the Bath Novella-in-Flash Award. This year another novella, *The Twisted Wheel*, finished runner-up in the same contest, and will be published soon. His other publications include *The Privilege of Rain* (based on his experiences as a Writer-in-Residence in a prison and shortlisted for the Ted Hughes Award). A former newspaper reporter, and toilet cleaner in a legendary Amsterdam night-club, David now teaches at the University of Chichester, and makes fires on his allotment.

Hilary Taylor grew up in Suffolk and Hampshire, and is a graduate of Edinburgh University. She now lives in Suffolk, where she taught for almost twenty years. Her short fiction has been published in magazines and anthologies and online, and has won prizes in the Bath Short Story Award, Flash500 and Writing Magazine. A previous flash fiction was shortlisted for the Bridport Prize in 2015. Her debut novel, *Sea Defences*, set on the fragile Norfolk coast, will be published by Lightning Books in January 2023, and she is currently working on a novel inspired by an intriguing family mystery. Twitter: @hilarytaylor00

Cath Wills lives in beautiful South Devon. She has raised three children and works as a teaching assistant. When she has time, Cath enjoys visiting Iron Age forts and has a fascination with all kinds of archaeology. But poetry comes first when time is spare, and she is inspired by the hidden aspects of us and our surroundings. Having worked a lot with children with special needs she is sympathetic to the voices that feel unheard. She has been writing and studying poetry since she was a child but has only recently felt brave enough to begin submitting her work.